The Autobiography of
HARRY S. TRUMAN

The Autobiography of
HARRY S. TRUMAN

Edited by Robert H. Ferrell

COLORADO ASSOCIATED UNIVERSITY PRESS

*While the portions of this work created by the editor
have been copyrighted it should be noted
that Mr. Truman's writings have been dedicated to
the people of the United States and are therefore
in the public domain.*

I have been reading a book about me . . . This book is supposed to be an educational one for young people. It contains more misstatements and false quotations than it contains facts and true statements from people purported to have been interviewed.

I've seen several books and pamphlets about my life, career, ambitions and accomplishments and most of them contain glaring errors. If Herodotus, Thucydides, Tacitus, Plutarch, Greene, Guizot, Mc-Cauley [sic], The Rise and Fall of the Roman Empire *are no more factual than the stories about me so far, then history and biography are just lies and reporters' readable stories and not facts. I've read somewhere that Herodotus said a good historian makes the facts fit the event to make good reading.*

To save too many knowing spreaders of misinformation from going to hell on the present biography I guess I'll have to state the few interesting facts of my life without the introspective trimmings with which most so-called writers and half-baked essayists clutter up the printed page. . . .

Contents

Foreword

The Autobiography of Harry S. Truman consists primarily of
one large "core" manuscript together with several smaller
autobiographical accounts, all in the president's handwriting. The result, one hopes, is a readable and instructive description and—because the late president was an imagina-
tive, thoughtful person—an analysis of how a small boy in
western Missouri became president of the United States.

In the early years of his adult life, and well into middle
age, at least until the age of fifty, Harry S. Truman never
had the slightest idea that he would achieve the presidency, and it is instructive to observe how remote the nation's highest political office seemed from him. As a youth
in Independence, a young bank clerk in Kansas City, and
then a farmer on a big farm near Grandview, Truman
thought about the affairs of his town, of Jackson County,
or his farm. He thought a good deal about the principles of
Masonry, and not merely joined the lodge in nearby
Belton in 1909 but next year organized a lodge in Grandview and became its first master, and took an intense interest in Masonry for the rest of his long life. When the
First World War opened in 1914 he did not see any imme-
diate dangers to his orderly ways, nor during his two years
of military service after the United States entered the war
did he anticipate any sort of political career. There is a
piquant observation in one of his later letters of how during a leave in Paris in early 1919 he stood outside the Hotel
Crillon and watched President Woodrow Wilson walk
down the steps after a conference inside. At that moment
no one—Wilson, Truman, anyone—could have imagined
that the thirty-five-year-old captain with the roundish

steel spectacles would reach the pinnacle of American and world authority a quarter century later, and preside over another peace, this one at least equal in importance to the Peace of Paris that so preoccupied Wilson in 1919. And Truman would negotiate a peace not merely with a resurgent Germany but with one of the apparently faithful allies of 1914-1918, Imperial Japan.

The rise of Truman to public prominence was very slow, and perhaps it was natural that he would write nothing of an autobiographical sort, about the course of his own life, until years later when his political career, begun with a county office in 1923, turned toward the national scene. The first evidence he gave of a sense of participation in history came in the early hours of May 14, 1934 when, alone in the Pickwick Hotel in Kansas City, he took up some hotel stationery and wrote of some of the influences on his life, including his World War service, influences that had led to the announcement he was to make that morning that he was running for the office of United States senator from Missouri.

A second evidence of the prominence that would envelope Harry S. Truman of Independence, Missouri came when he received the vice presidential nomination at the Democratic national convention in Chicago in the summer of 1944. If it had not been for the intensely busy weeks and months that followed, when the Democratic vice presidential nominee went around the country speaking for himself and for his chief, President Franklin D. Roosevelt, Truman surely would have written another autobiographical account—for in the summer of 1944 he knew that this nomination meant in effect the presidency: Roosevelt would win a fourth term, and the president could not survive that term. After taking office as vice president, Truman sometime between January 20, 1945 and April 12 again resorted to autobiography, and wrote down the history of his life from graduation from Independence High School in 1901 to the vice presidency, this in a huge manuscript of fifty-nine pages, all in his bold-faced hand. This manuscript of perhaps 12,000 words constitutes the core manuscript of the present book.

The third time Truman looked back over his life and wrote down his inner thoughts came in the year 1951, or perhaps it was early 1952, when his journalistic friend William Hillman was putting together a book of diary entries, memoranda, speeches, commentaries on this and that, interleafed with color and black-and-white pictures by the photographer Alfred Wagg. One morning the president gave Hillman a sheaf of handwritten notes he had composed the night before, comprising an account of his early years, from ages two until eighteen, and in subsequent days he wrote out more accounts, four more of them, taking his life through the vice presidency. Hillman published this material in *Mr. President* (New York: Farrar, Straus and Young, 1952), and it has constituted a sort of quarry, from which came four pieces for the present book.

Then there was a memorandum, written for Hillman early in 1952, about the Pendergast machine in Kansas City, a sober telling of Truman's connection with the machine, of how it was possible to work with the machine and not be soiled by it. And a memo about the vice presidential nomination, written after the former chairman of the Democratic national committee, Frank Walker, came in to see the president early in January 1950 with a story of the byzantine maneuvers by which the party leaders in 1944, anticipating Roosevelt's death, shunted aside the then vice president, Henry A. Wallace, and avoided supporting the "assistant president" and former senator from South Carolina and associate justice of the supreme court, James F. Byrnes, whose cause they deemed hopeless because Byrnes had antagonized the leaders of American labor, and gave their support to a man they knew and respected—Truman. In the Truman Library in Independence is a handwritten draft of a "farewell address" to the American people, different from the address the president delivered for that purpose, and it summarizes the achievements of the Truman presidency. A little speech, read from manuscript notes to the citizens of Independence on February 5, 1953, sets out the ex-president's feelings and emotions upon returning to his home town. The *Autobiography* concludes with some of the retired president's random thoughts about politics and the purposes of public life—the sort of subjects with which he occupied his time in retirement until his death on December 26, 1972.

These, then, have been the building blocks of *The Autobiography of Harry S. Truman.*

One aspect about the *Autobiography* is worth stressing, namely, that because it is based entirely on manuscript material, in the president's hand, it is not something invented by individuals who did not know what he desired—or did—or concluded from what he did. There can be no doubt that the *Autobiography* is Harry S. Truman himself.

Acknowledgments

The Harry S. Truman Library in Independence is a very attractive institution, for the library is convenient in ways that many such places are not. The search room contains all the books a reader needs to identify personages or look up the details of events, and there are runs of pertinent periodicals. Nearby is a library within a library; here are reference books without end, anything related to the life and times of President Truman. The manuscript records are carefully arranged, so that with the simplest of research aids it is possible to run down the box numbers and indeed the folder names of manuscript items. As for the staff, they are helpful in ways seldom encountered elsewhere, for they take as their roles the simple assistance of researchers. The management of the library is not by a series of bureaucratic rules but by simplicity. No one puts a long form under the noses of researchers before they can use the library; everything is easy to understand. From the director on down, helpful informality is the rule. And so thanks go to Benedict K. Zobrist, the director; George Curtis, assistant director; Vicky Alexander, Dennis E. Bilger, Patty Bressman, Mildred L. Carol, Harry Clark, John Curry, Diane Farris, Niel M. Johnson, Philip D. Lagerquist, Erwin J. Mueller, Warren Ohrvall, Doris Pesek, Elizabeth Safly and Pauline Testerman.

Mrs. Howard Carvin offered gracious hospitality, including many delicious meals, at 400 North Delaware Street.

Wendy Jensen, Libby Gitlitz, and Debbie Chase ably did the typing, and told me, with suitable grins from behind their typewriters, that they had come to know Harry S. Truman better.

Acknowledgments

John M. Hollingsworth was the cartographer for the map of Independence.

I am grateful indeed for the assistance of Mrs. Ardis Haukenberry.

Frederick R. Rinehart and Bruce Campbell of the Colorado Associated University Press were immensely helpful in planning the present book. Rick imaginatively handled all sorts of things in an editorial way, and Bruce's inspired design makes a book pleasant to behold and easy to read.

Lila and Carolyn offered their usual support, which lightens all tasks.

R.H.F.
Independence, Mo.
July 4, 1980

CHAPTER I

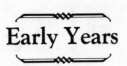

Early Years

THE WHITE HOUSE
WASHINGTON

My first memory is that of
chasing a frog around the
backyard in Cass County, Mo.
Grandmother Young watched
the performance and thought
it very funny that a two year
old could slap his knees and
laugh so loudly at a jumping frog.
Then I remember another
incident at the same farm
when my mother dropped me
from an upstairs window into
the arms of my Uncle Harrison
Young, who had come to see
the new baby, my brother Vivian.

My first memory is that of chasing a frog around the back yard in Cass County, Missouri. Grandmother Young watched the performance and thought it very funny that a two-year-old could slap his knees and laugh so loudly at a jumping frog.

Then I remember another incident at the same farm when my mother dropped me from an upstairs window into the arms of my Uncle Harrison Young, who had come to see the new baby, my brother Vivian.

I was named for . . . Harrison Young. I was given the diminutive Harry and, so that I could have two initials in my given name, the letter S was added. My Grandfather Truman's name was Anderson Shippe Truman and my Grandfather Young's name was Solomon Young, so I received the S for both of them.

I was very fond of my Uncle Harrison. He was a big man a little over six feet in height and he weighed 201 pounds. He was as strong as a wrestler and was very good looking.

He remained a bachelor all his life and was a good story teller. He was also a genius at games of chance, checkers, chess, poker, pitch, cooncan and sevenup.

He lived on the farm with my Grandmother Young, raised fine cattle, hogs and sheep. It was my custom and my brother's also to spend a lot of time on the old home farm with Uncle Harrison and our Grandmother.

The old uncle was very fond of both of us, particularly of me because I was named for him. He taught me how to play checkers, sevenup and cooncan and would tell me stories of his adventures in the West and in southern Jackson County, Missouri in his younger days.

Wheat, corn, oats and clover were raised on the farm. On one occasion when I was on the farm the big white field corn was just right for making corn pudding and roasting ears. I told the uncle I was going to the field and

3

"My father bought me a shetland pony about this time . . . one day coming down the north road toward the house I fell off the pony and had to walk about a half mile to the house. My father said that a boy who was not able to stay on a pony at a walk ought to walk himself. Mamma thought I was badly mistreated but I wasn't . . . I learned a lesson." [The parents of Harry S. Truman—Martha Ellen and John Anderson Truman.]

get an armful of green corn so we could have a corn pudding. The cook knew how to make an excellent one.

When I started out Uncle Harrison was sitting in the yard under an old pine tree and he asked me where I was going. I told him and he asked me if I knew what was the record number of ears of corn a man had eaten at one sitting. Of course I didn't and he proceeded to tell me about a pal of his who had made the record on a bet by eating thirteen roasting ears. Then this pal cultivated a severe stomach ache and had to send for the doctor. The doctor worked over him most of the night and then told him he'd better send for the preacher and do a little praying because medical aid was at an end.

Well the man was in such pain he finally sent for the parson and the good man prayed for him; he was very earnestly told that he'd have to pray for himself. He told the preacher that he was not a praying man and didn't think he could do it. However the extremity was so great that he finally decided to make the attempt.

So he got down on his knees in the old-fashioned revival manner and this was his petition to the Almighty:

"Oh Lord, I am in great pain and misery. I have eaten thirteen roasting ears and I don't seem to be able to take care of them. I am praying to you for help, and Lord I'm not like the damned howling church members in the amen corner; if you'll relieve me of seven of these damned ears of corn I'll try to wrastle around the other six."

We moved from the Cass County farm to the old home of my mother's father in Jackson County. Grandfather Truman lived with us and he made a favorite out of me, as did my Grandfather Young.

I can remember when my Truman grandfather died. All three of his daughters were present, Aunt Ella, Aunt Emma and Aunt Matt. I was four years old and was very curious about what was happening. Grandpa Truman was a grand man and petted me a great deal. He was a strong Baptist and violently anti-Catholic.

I was also a great favorite of Grandpa Young's. He'd take me to the Belton fair with him and I'd sit in the judges' stand and watch the races—grandpa was a judge.

My brother Vivian was two years my junior and he had lovely long curls. Grandpa and I cut off his curls one day by putting him in a highchair out on the south porch. Mamma was angry enough to spank us both, but she had such respect for her father that she only frowned at him. One day after the hair-cutting episode I sat on the edge of a chair in front of the mirror to comb my hair—I fell off the chair backwards and broke my collarbone—my first but not my last broken bone. Later in this same room I was eating a peach and swallowed the seed. Almost choked to death but mamma pushed the seed down my throat with her finger and I lived to tell about it.

Vivian and I used to play in the south pasture—a beautiful meadow in bluegrass. At the end of the grove was a mudhole. This grove was row on row of beautiful maple trees, a quarter of a mile long and six rows wide. We had a little red wagon which we took with us on our adventures in the pasture. We finally wound up at the mudhole with a neighbor boy about our age and I loaded Vivian and John Chancellor into the little wagon, hauled them into the mudhole—and *upset* the wagon. What a spanking I received. I can feel it yet! Every stitch of clothes on all three of us had to be changed, scrubbed and dried, and so did we!

My father bought me a Shetland pony about this time, and a beautiful little saddle—my brother's granddaughter has the saddle now. I'd ride with my father on my little Shetland and he on his big horse. He'd lead my pony and I felt perfectly safe—but one day coming down the north road toward the house I fell off the pony and had to walk

"My brother Vivian was two years my junior and he had lovely long curls. Grandpa and I cut off his curls one day by putting him in a highchair out on the south porch." [Vivian and Harry Truman, aged four and six.]

about half a mile to the house. My father said that a boy who was not able to stay on a pony at a walk ought to walk himself. Mamma thought I was badly mistreated but I wasn't, in spite of my crying all the way to the house. I learned a lesson.

When I was five and Vivian was three we were presented with a sister—Mary Jane, named for her Grandmother Truman. We heard her cry upstairs and thought we had a new pet until our father told us we had a new sister.

When I was six, Vivian three, and Mary one year old, we moved to Independence. Mamma was anxious we should have town schooling. About this time my eyes became a problem and mamma took me to Dr. Thompson in Kansas City. Dr. Thompson was the brother-in-law of Dr. Charlie Lester, the son of the family physician in Civil War times, and himself the family doctor by succession. Glasses were fitted by Dr. Thompson and I've worn practically the same prescription ever since. When I first put the glasses on I saw things and saw print I'd never seen before. I learned to read when I was five but never could see the fine print. I've been "fine printed" many a time since I've been able to read it.

When I was eight I started to school at the Noland School on South Liberty Street. My first grade teacher was Miss Myra Ewing, a grand woman. That first year in school made a profound impression on me. I learned to get along with my classmates and also learned a lot from Appleton's *First Reader*, learned how to add and subtract, and stood in well with my teacher.

In my second school year Miss Minnie Ward was my teacher. She was a good teacher and a lovely woman.

Along in January my brother and I had a terrible case of diphtheria—no antitoxin in those days. They gave us ipecac and whiskey. I've hated the smell of both ever since.

The family sent Mary Jane to the farm so she wouldn't catch the disease. Old Letch, the husband of our cook and washwoman, Caroline Simpson, took Mary Jane to the farm in a big farm wagon, driving a fine team of horses. It took nearly all day to make the trip, and it was not known for two more days, when old Letch returned.

Aunt Caroline (aunty we called her) and her husband Letch worked for us from the time we moved to Independence. There were five children in aunty's family—an older girl named Amy whom I never saw, Sam, Horace, Claude and Delsie. Sam (Fat Sam) afterwards became the fireman at the county home and stayed there until he died. Horace went insane, as did his father, Letch. Claude became an efficient Pullman porter and died on the job. Delsie is still alive, a cripple from her teens.

My brother and I recovered from our illness and I went to summer school to catch up to the third grade. A new school house had been built in the meantime—the Columbian. Next door to the school lived a lovely old lady who had helped nurse me to health after my terrible experience with diphtheria. I was paralyzed for six months after the throat disease left me, and my mother wheeled me around in a baby buggy. My arms, legs and throat were of no use, but I recovered and went back to school and skipped the third grade. Then went to the fifth with Aunt Nannie Wallace as the teacher. She was a wonder of a teacher—had been at it for thirty years and knew her job. . . .

After a seventh grade course at the Columbian School we all went to high school at the old Ott School on North Liberty Street. We had wonderful teachers, Prof. Palmer, Miss Hardin (afterwards Mrs. Palmer), Miss Tillie Brown, Miss Sallie Brown, Miss McDonald and Prof. Patrick, Prof. Bryant and Prof. Baldwin, superintendent of schools. All of them made a contribution to the knowledge and

"*After a seventh grade course at the Columbian School we all went to high school at the old Ott School on North Liberty Street.*" [Harry Truman, aged thirteen.]

character of the students. It was a great class. Besides the present First Lady, there were in it Charles G. Ross, a great journalist and press secretary to the president, a great physician and surgeon, Dr. Elmer Twyman, son and grandson of great doctors. His father was our doctor in the diphtheria case, along with Dr. Charlie Lester. I slammed the cellar door on my foot and cut off the end of my big toe on the left foot. Mamma held it in place until Dr. Tom Twyman, Elmer's father, put some iodoform on it and it stayed put and got well!

In 1896 we moved to a nice house at Waldo Avenue and River Boulevard. Before I leave the house on Crysler Street, I remember my father's discovery of gas in the back lot where he was drilling a water well. Water was struck at 140 feet but it was sulphur water and the stock wouldn't drink it. So a deeper well was drilled in the same hole. Two strata of gas and one of oil were hit. We had the old house piped for gas, put in a gas tank, and for a while had an ideal setup. Then the oil choked off the gas and my father traded for the Waldo Avenue property. There was a cupola or tower on the northwest corner of the Crysler Street house and when Cleveland was elected in 1892, the rooster weathervane on top of the tower was properly decorated and my father rode a gray horse in the torchlight victory parade.

There were a lot of new boys and girls in the Waldo Avenue neighborhood. We had many a grand time with them. In the Spanish-American War we organized a .22 rifle company, elected a captain and marched and countermarched, camped out in the woods just a block or two north of our house, and had a grand time. Not one of the boys was over fourteen.

On White Oak Street, a block south, lived two Houchens boys, sons of a preacher. At the east end of White Oak at Union Street lived two Chiles boys—Henry

"In 1896 we moved to a nice house at Waldo Avenue and River Boulevard."

and Morton. Across Waldo at Woodland College was Paul Bryant. Two doors east on Waldo was Jim Wright, and next door east on Waldo were five girls and three boys— the Burruses.

Down on Delaware, two blocks east of River Boulevard, lived the Paxtons and the Wallaces, with the Sawyers on the corner of Waldo and Delaware Street. The grand times we had! Halloween parties and all sorts of meetings after school, making bridges by Caesar's plans and discussing what we'd like to be when grown up. We published a high school paper in 1901, called *The Gleam* for Tennyson's "Follow the Gleam." It is still published by the Independence High School after fifty years.

Not of the sunlight,
Not of the moonlight,
Not of the starlight!
O young Mariner,
Down to the haven,
Call your companions,
Launch your vessel,
And crowd your canvas,
And, ere it vanishes
Over the margin
After it, follow it,
Follow The Gleam.
TENNYSON.

"We published a high school paper in 1901, called The Gleam for Tennyson's 'Follow the Gleam.' It is still published by the Independence High School after fifty years."

The Independence High School graduating class of 1901. Seventeen-year-old Harry S. Truman is in the last row, fourth from the left.

CHAPTER II

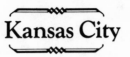

Kansas City

When I graduated from high school in May, 1901, it was expected by the family and by me that there would be some chance for more education. Difficulties overtook us which resulted in the loss of the family farm of 160 acres and of the home place at Waldo and River Boulevard in Independence. It was necessary that some addition be made to the family income. So I got a job as timekeeper on a railroad construction outfit under L. J. Smith. He was building a double track for the Santa Fe Railroad from a little place named Eton to Sheffield, a suburb of Kansas City. My salary was thirty-five dollars a month and board. There were three construction camps about five miles apart. It was my job to check the men at each of these camps twice daily. I was furnished with a tricycle car. Its power was by hand and I furnished the power.

The workmen were hobos and they worked from payday to payday to get enough money for one weekend drunk. Payday was every two weeks. If a man drew his pay under the two weeks' time he was discounted ten percent. Daily pay was fifteen cents an hour for ten hours a day. A team and dump wagon received thirty-five cents an hour for ten hours a day. Blacksmiths, cooks and specialists received seventeen and one-half cents an hour or a dollar seventy-five a day.

On Saturday, every two weeks, I sat in some saloon either in Independence or Sheffield and signed checks for all who'd worked two weeks and who wanted to be paid off. Some of the men only drew pay once a month or sometimes once in six months. These men were very few in number and were usually farmers who owned teams and wagons. They saved their money. Hobos only used money for one purpose—to buy whiskey at the bar where the check was cashed until all the money was gone. After the biweekly libation was slept off, most of 'em were back on the job Monday morning to start in for another two weeks.

After working some eight or ten months for the railroad contractor, the job ended by being completed and I went to work for the Kansas City *Star* "wrapping singles" in the mailing department at nine dollars a week—a raise in pay. Then one of my friends came along early in 1903 or late in 1902 and I went to work in the basement of the National Bank of Commerce at Tenth and Walnut, Kansas City, Missouri, as a clerk at thirty-five dollars a month. At that time we lived at 2108 Park Avenue in Kansas City. My brother and I worked at the bank and my father worked at an elevator in the east bottoms. In 1904, my father traded the house at 2108 Park for an equity in 80 acres in Henry County, Missouri, and late in 1904 the family moved to Clinton. I went to board at 1314 Troost Avenue with some of the bank boys. A good woman named Trow ran the boarding house. We lived two in a room and paid five dollars a week for room, breakfast and dinner. For lunch we paid ten cents to a box lunch place on East Eighth Street—and we stayed in good condition physically too. Mrs. Trow was a cook you read of but seldom see and the box lunch was a balanced ration before vitamins were ever heard of.

Early in 1905 I quit the National Bank of Commerce and went to work for the Union National Bank. I'd improved my financial position in the National Bank of Commerce by some twenty-five dollars a month. But the Union National gave me seventy-five dollars a month to do exactly the same kind of work I was doing at the Commerce for sixty dollars, so I moved. It was a much pleasanter place to work. The chief clerk and the vice president in charge of the help at the Union National were

"*I went to work in the basement of the National Bank of Commerce at Tenth and Walnut, Kansas City, Missouri, as a clerk at thirty-five dollars a month.*" [Presumably the young bank clerk.]

kind and sympathetic while the chief clerk and the vice president at the Commerce were just the opposite.

The vice president at the Commerce who hired and fired the help was a fellow named Charles H. Moore. His job was to do the official bawling out. He was an artist at it. He could have humiliated the nerviest man in the world. Anyway, all the boys in the Commerce Zoo were afraid of him, as were all the tellers and bookkeepers. He was never so happy as when he could call some poor inoffensive little clerk up before him in the grand lobby of the biggest bank west of the Mississippi and tell him how dumb and inefficient he was because he'd sent a check belonging in the remittance of the State Bank of Oakland, Kansas, to Ogden, Utah. He would always remember that trivial mistake when that clerk asked for a raise. Raises were hard to get and if a man got an additional five dollars on his monthly pay he was a go-getter, because he'd out-talked the bawler-out and had taken something from the tightest-wad bank president on record. The president's name was Dr. W. S. Woods. He'd been a country doctor at Fulton, Missouri, and had finally gone into finance, became the owner of the National Bank of Commerce at Kansas City, the Clay County State Bank at Excelsior Springs and the Woods and Ruby Bank at Golden, Colorado—besides a lot of other commercial enterprises. There are dozens of stories about his close counting of the nickels and the pennies— but if he chose to back a man, he stayed with him through thick and thin if that man had energy and character.

I wasn't long at the Union National Bank until I was getting $100 a month—a magnificent salary in Kansas City in 1905.

[Kansas City, so President Truman wrote to the publisher of the Kansas City *Star* in 1950, was a fascinating place at the turn of the century.] Ninth Street was double-track, Main northbound and Delaware southbound. Independence Avenue cars were green, . . . Ninth Street cars were red, and made connection with the "Dummy Line" which went to Independence. The crossing watchman . . . once pulled my mother back from the curb in front of the C.&A. office and when she turned on him to tell him off he said, "Only saving your life, madam, only saving your life." He was, too, for he pulled her back in time to miss a westbound car. We, of course, wanted to go east.

. . . My Aunt Laura lived at Third and Campbell. She was voted the most beautiful girl in Jackson County and awarded the prize, but as is usual in such cases there was a protest. She gave the prize back to the judges and she was again given it unanimously. Her married name was Mrs. W. B. Eberhart. Two of her daughters are still living, and will confirm what I'm saying.

Again, at Ninth and Main and Delaware just north of the C.&A. office was the Soda Fountain and Candy Shop of Jesse James, Jr. I was a pupil at Spalding's Commercial College in the New York Life Building in 1901 and early 1902, studying debit and credit and Pittman shorthand. Carfare and a quarter for lunch was all I received when I left home. I also took a music lesson from Mrs. E. C. White on these trips.

Well on one occasion I stopped in Jesse's place and had an ice cream soda—five cents. When I'd finished it I found I had no nickel, only a car ticket home. Jesse said, "Oh that's all right, pay when you come in again." I paid the nickel the next day! My father stood for honesty.

My Grandmother Young saw the flood of 1844 and we took her to see the flood of 1903. Her comment was, "This flood is no greater, but more property is destroyed." She was a grand old Kentuckian, and she had the most beautiful red hair.

In reading of the growth of the city I can't help but remember the part the owner of the *Star* had in placing a cemetery at Washington Park and stopping the city's east-ward growth. Placing the Union Station where it is cut the city in half and almost ruined the central business district. . . . The Grand and the old Orpheum on West Ninth Street with the old blood-and-thunder Gilliss were all we had from 1900 until the Willis Wood was built.

The Four Cohans, Primrose and Dockstader, Williams and Walker, "East Lynne," Chauncey Alcott—all came to the Grand.

Marguerite Sylva, Sarah Bernhardt, Eddie Foy, Chick Sale, and numerous other of the great vaudeville stars came to the old Ninth Street Orpheum. . . . the great Weber and Fields appearance in Convention Hall with Lillian Russell at her best, Nat Wills and all the other great of burlesque.

As for Kansas City's musical taste . . . there was "Parsifal," "Lohengrin," "Cavalleria Rusticana," "Pagliacci," "Les Huguenots," all by the Metropolitan Opera in Convention Hall.

There was Paderewski, who taught me how to play his famous minuet, Rosenthal, Augusta Cotlow, and the greatest of them all, Joseph Lhévinne, who came to Convention Hall. And Vladimir de Pachmann, and all those named above who came to the Shubert. There were Donald Brian, Joseph Cawthorn and two other stars in "The Girl from Utah," famous for the song, "They'll Never Believe Me." Marlowe and Sothern in "The Taming of the Shrew."

"The Spring Maid," a lovely musical show, and many others.

Richard Mansfield at the Willis Wood in "Dr. Jekyll and Mr. Hyde." I was afraid to go home after seeing it. Walker Whiteside in "Richard III," Sir Henry Irving and Ellen Terry in "The Merchant of Venice," "Julius Caesar," and "Hamlet."

Then there was the old Woodward Stock Company at the Auditorium. They played "Hamlet," "Romeo and Juliet," "Midsummer Night's Dream," and again at the Shubert, Robert Mantell in "Richelieu."

CHAPTER III

Back on the Farm

"My grandmother . . . was a grand old lady. Had helped make my grandfather a successful man." [Grandmother Young, aged eighty-one.]

I n June of . . . [1905] Captain George R. Collins decided to start a National Guard battery of light artillery in Kansas City. Some of the boys in the bank were going into it. I was twenty-one years old in May of that year and could do as I pleased. So I joined the battery. After reading all the books obtainable in the Independence and Kansas City libraries on history and government from Egypt to U.S.A., I came to the conclusion that every citizen should know something about military, finance or banking, and agriculture. All my heroes or great leaders were somewhat familiar with one or the other, or all three. So I started my grass roots military education by joining a National Guard battery, June 14, 1905. In August we went to our first encampment at Cape Girardeau, Missouri. It was quite an experience. We went to St. Louis in a day coach on the Missouri Pacific and then by steamboat down the Mississippi. I learned a lot about public relations and private ones too. There were several camps after that one—at St. Joseph, where we camped in three feet of water in the fairgrounds and a tent was struck by lightning, killing a man or two—at Fort Riley, Kansas, where I was made a corporal. I still have the warrant framed. It was the biggest promotion I ever received and I've had 'em all up to colonel and vice president of the U.S.A.

After the family moved to Clinton, I spent weekends down there and at the old home farm at Grandview where my maternal grandmother and the old bachelor uncle, for whom I was named, lived. The uncle wanted to move back to town so he made a proposition to my father and mother to come back to the old home place and live. I took the word to them at Clinton and urged them to move. They agreed to accept and I agreed to quit the bank and go to work on the farm if they did move. So in 1906 we all moved to the old home place at Grandview. My grandmother was eighty-eight years old at the time but as hale and hearty as a woman of fifty. She was a grand old lady. Had helped make my grandfather a successful man. She was a good Baptist, a strong sympathizer with the Confederate States of America and an Indian fighter on her own. She has told me a great many stories of conditions in Jackson County in the 1840s. My grandfather ran a wagon train from Westport and Independence to Salt Lake City and San Francisco from 1844 to the late sixties and my grandmother kept the five thousand-acre Jackson County farms going. She not only raised her own children—seven of them to be grown—two died as children—but she raised a couple of nephews and numerous slave children and neighbor orphans. She had the most beautiful red hair I've ever seen, and a kindly, benevolent attitude to those she liked. If she didn't like a person, he didn't have any difficulty in finding it out. She was kind and considerate to those who worked for her, but she stood for no foolishness and she had a way of keeping people in their proper places which I've never seen equalled. For instance, after I'd joined the Missouri National Guard in 1905, I went out one weekend to show her my new Guard uniform—beautiful blue with red stripes down the trouser legs and red piping on the cuffs and a red fourragère over the shoulder. She looked me over and I knew I was going to catch it. She said, "Harry, this is the first time since 1863 that a blue uniform has been in this house. Don't bring it here again." I didn't.

In the difficulties along the Missouri-Kansas border old Jim Lane, a Kansas hero, had burned her house, killed four hundred of her hogs, cut the hams out and let the carcasses lie to rot. On top of that he forced her to make biscuits for the men until all her fingers were blistered. Old Jim was on his way to plunder and Osceola, Missouri at that time. That caused Quantrill to go to Lawrence for

"*. . . after I'd joined the Missouri National Guard in 1905, I went out one weekend to show [Grandmother Young] my new Guard uniform . . . She looked me over and I knew I was going to catch it. She said, 'Harry, this is the first time since 1863 that a blue uniform has been in this house. Don't bring it here again.' I didn't.*"

reprisals. Old Jim's a hero in the history books and Quantrill's a villain. It all depends on who writes the histories. The Adamses and the New England historians made a crook and an atheist out of Thomas Jefferson, until honest research proved 'em in error (to put it mildly).

Well, I went to the farm in 1906 and stayed there, contrary to all the prophecies, until April 1917, really until August 5, 1917. It was a great experience. Wish I'd kept a diary. It was my job to help my father and brother feed the livestock, sometimes milk a couple of cows, then help my mother get breakfast. After breakfast we'd go to the fields. In spring and fall there'd be plowing to do. We had gang plows made by the Emerson Plow Company—two twelve-inch plows on a three-wheeled frame. It required four horses or mules to pull it and if an early start was had, about five acres could be broken up in a day—not an eight-hour one but in, say, ten or twelve hours. In the spring when the weather was cool and the teams could be kept moving the time was shorter. That sort of a plow is the best demonstration of horsepower, pounds, feet, minutes. Sometimes the horses gave out and then the power was off until a rest was had. Riding one of these plows all day, day after day, gives one time to think. I've settled all the ills of mankind in one way and another while riding along seeing that each animal pulled his part of the load. Sometimes in the early part of the year it would be so cold that walking was in order to keep warm, even when a sweater, two coats and an overcoat were worn.

It was always my job to plant the corn, sow the wheat and run the binder to cut the wheat and oats. I usually pitched hay up to my father on the stack also. My father hated a crooked corn row or a skipped place in a wheat field. We had no crooked rows and our wheat and oat fields had no bare places in them and when the binder had finished a wheat or oat field there were no uncut strips in

"Riding one of these plows all day, day after day, gives one time to think. I've settled all the ills of mankind in one way and another while riding along seeing that each animal pulled his part of the load." [Harry Truman on a cultivator, about 1910.]

the field. We used a rotation system in our farm program. We'd plant corn after clover. Starting with wheat we'd sow clover on the wheat field in the spring and usually get a crop of clover hay that fall. The next year we'd spread all the manure from the farm and the little town adjoining it on the clover field. Nearly every family in the little town of 300 people had a cow or two and a horse. My father and I bought a manure spreader and kept it busy all the time when we were not doing other necessary things. We'd break the clover field up in the fall and plant corn the next spring, sow oats in the corn stubble the next spring and wheat after oats. It would take five years to make the complete rotation but it worked most successfully. We increased the wheat yield from thirteen to nineteen bushels—the oats from eight to fifty bushels and the corn from thirty-five to seventy bushels to the acre. Besides these increased yields in the grain crops we always had two excellent hay crops and at least one seed crop from the clover, so my practical education in farm management took place in those ten years.

In January, 1909, I put in an application for membership in Belton Lodge 450 A.F. & A.M. They voted me in and I took the first degree in February, and in March finished up the third. That spring and summer I spent teaching the plow horses all the Masonic lectures. I also found that by counting the number of turns my land wheel made on the gang plow I could measure the acreage of the field I was plowing, so every night there was an accurate check on the amount plowed.

I became very much interested in the work of the Masons and put in a great deal of time on it, so that in December, 1909, I was elected junior warden of Belton Lodge. Along in the summer of 1909 it was suggested that Grandview should have a lodge of its own, so after finding that it would require a certain number to start a lodge in Grandview, some of us went to work on it and in the summer of 1910 succeeded in obtaining enough signers to start out a lodge under dispensation. When the grand lodge met in the fall of 1910 a charter was authorized. They made me the presiding officer under dispensation and then elected me in December to serve as the first master under the new charter. The organization has been very successful and a power for good in the community since that date.

In 1924 the grand master of the state appointed me his deputy for the Fifty-ninth District. In 1930 the Hon. William R. Gentry, grand master at the time, started me in the grand lodge line by appointment and in 1940 the grand lodge session in St. Louis on the last Tuesday in

September elected me grand master. It is a high honor and one for which I was most grateful to my friends and brethren.

When we moved to Independence in 1890 my mother's first thought was to get us into a good Sunday school. The nearest church to our home, to which she was willing to take us, was the First Presbyterian, so we started to Sunday school there immediately. We went regularly and learned all the good stories of the Old and New Testaments. By the time I was twelve I'd read the whole book through twice and knew a lot of stories in it which were not particularly stressed in Sunday school—for instance, the final ending of old man Lot's march out of Sodom and David's terrible treatment of Uriah. But the greatest impression I received was the system of morals taught by Moses in the twentieth chapter of Exodus and the Sermon on the Mount as reported in the fifth, sixth and seventh chapters of the Gospel according to St. Matthew.

We were taught that punishment always followed transgression and my mother saw to it that it did. She kept a good switch and a slipper handy for application to the spot where most good could be accomplished on young anatomy. My father never did punish me except an occasional scolding, which hurt worse than a good spanking would have.

When I was eighteen I joined the Baptist Church and have kept my membership in that church ever since. My membership now is in the Grandview Baptist Church where it has been for forty years. I'm not very much impressed with men who publicly parade their religious beliefs. My old grandfather used to say that when he heard his neighbor pray too loudly in public he always went home and locked his smokehouse. I've always believed that religion is something to live by and not to talk about. I'm a Baptist because I think that sect gives the common man the shortest and most direct approach to God. I've never thought the Almighty is greatly interested in pomp and circumstance, because if He is He wouldn't be interested in "the sparrow" alluded to in St. Matthew's Gospel. Religious stuffed shirts are just as bad or worse than political ones in my opinion.

When my mother started us to Sunday school she gave us a chance to meet the other children in Independence. I met a very beautiful little lady with lovely blue eyes and the prettiest golden curls I've ever seen. We went through Sunday school, grade school, high school and we're still going along hand in hand. She was my sweetheart and ideal when I was a little boy—and she still is. We have a daughter who takes after (that is the way we put it in Missouri) her mother and, of course, that makes me very happy.

Along in 1910 we had a very bitter political campaign over the election of an eastern judge in Jackson County. After the smoke blew away my father was appointed road overseer for the south half of Washington Township. It was quite a job. He had to fix bridges and culverts, fill up mudholes and try to help everyone in the neighborhood get to and away from his farm in bad weather. There were only a few miles of macadam roads in the township. All the rest were dirt. It was my father's job to collect the poll tax and work it out. A man could work three days on the road or he could pay the road overseer three dollars and let his road work be done by proxy. One day's work with a team of horses would also give him a clean bill of health. It was my father's policy actually to work the roads for the money. Some of the overseers collected the money and seldom worked. The county court sometimes appropriated special sums for culverts, small bridges and mudholes, which the road overseer spent and for which he turned in bills, receiving county warrants. Sometimes these warrants

"When my mother started us to Sunday school she gave us a chance to meet the other children in Independence. I met a very beautiful little lady with lovely blue eyes and the prettiest golden curls I've ever seen. She was my sweetheart and ideal when I was a little boy—and she still is." [Bess Wallace, the future first lady, at ages four and thirteen.]

were good for cash, but most of the time they were promises to pay. They drew 6 percent interest when they were presented for registration. The banks would discount them and hope to cash them when enough taxes were collected to make them good. At one time the county had more than $2 million in outstanding warrants but this was much later.

My father was a very honorable man. If he guaranteed a horse in a horse trade that guarantee was as good as a bond. If he agreed to do a day's work for a certain amount of money he'd give good measure on the work. He always expected the people who worked for him to give him a day's work for a day's pay—and woe to a loafer. He made the poll tax workers work for the county just as they worked for themselves. While they'd beef about it on the job they'd go home and brag about how old man Truman gave the taxpayers a fair break. I was taught that the expenditure of public money is a public trust and I have never changed my opinion on that subject. No one ever received any public money for which I was responsible unless he gave honest service for it.

When my father passed away in 1914 I was appointed road overseer in his place and served until the presiding judge became dissatisfied because I gave the county too much for the money. In the meantime Congressman Borland appointed me postmaster at Grandview. I let a widow woman who was helping to raise and educate her younger sisters and brothers run the office as assistant postmaster and take the pay which amounted to about fifty dollars a month—a lot of money in those days. It would have paid two farmhands.

Along in 1915 I met a promoter by the name of Jerry Culbertson, through one of our farmer neighbors. This neighbor, a good man by the name of Tom Hughes, had been sheriff of Cass County at the same time that Jerry had been prosecuting attorney of the same county. Mr. Hughes had invested in several gold mines with Mr. Culbertson, none of which had made any returns on the investment.

Mr. Culbertson interested Mr. Hughes and me in a zinc and lead mine at Commerce, Oklahoma, and I undertook to run it, along with a red-haired hoisting engineer by the name of Bill Throop. Bill was all wool and a yard wide but we couldn't make our mine pay. He asked me to raise $2,500 and buy a drilling machine and go up north of Pitcher, Oklahoma and prospect the land up there for lead and zinc. But I'd already put all my ready money into the Commerce mine and couldn't raise the $2,500. If I'd done it we'd both be rolling in wealth today. The Commerce mine petered out and I lost $2,000. Mr. Culbertson then organized an oil company and Hughes and I were suckers enough to go into it. Some $200,000 was raised and leases were bought in Texas, Oklahoma and Kansas. At the time the war came we had a well down nine hundred feet on a 320-acre lease at Eureka, Kansas. I got all patriotic and joined the army. My partners got into a fuss and let that lease go to pot. Another company took it over and drilled a well on it and there was never a dry hole found on that 320 acres. It was the famous Teter Pool. If I'd stayed home and run my oil company I'd have been a millionaire. But I always did let ethics beat me out of money and I suppose I always will.

CHAPTER IV

The First World War

"When President Wilson declared war on April 6, 1917 . . . I was elected a first lieutenant. I had not expected to be more than a second lieutenant and would have been happy just to remain a sergeant."

I was stirred in heart and soul by the war messages of Woodrow Wilson, and since I'd joined the National Guard at twenty-one I thought I ought to go. I believe that the great majority of the country were stirred by the same flame that stirred me in those great days. I felt that I was a Galahad after the Grail and I'll never forget how my love cried on my shoulder when I told her I was going. That was worth a lifetime on this earth.

When President Wilson declared war on April 6, 1917, however, I helped to expand Batteries B and C into a regiment. At the organization of Battery F, I was elected a first lieutenant. I had not expected to be more than a second lieutenant and would have been happy just to remain a sergeant. I made arrangements for my sister and a good man we had on the farm to take over its operation and I set to work to be a field artillery man sure enough. It was some job. We were drilling every day from early in May as Missouri National Guard until the federal call on August 5 when we became known as the 129th Field Artillery of the 60th Brigade attached to the 35th Division. From May until August 5, 1917 we were known as the 2nd Missouri Field Artillery.

On September 26, 1917 we arrived at Camp Doniphan located just west of and adjoining Fort Sill, Oklahoma. My duties really piled up after we arrived at camp. Not only was it expected of me to do regular duty as a first lieutenant in Battery F but the colonel made me regimental canteen officer. I'd had no experience in merchandizing so I persuaded Captain Pete Allen who commanded Battery F to let me get Sergeant Edward Jacobson assigned to me to operate the canteen. We then got orders issued that each battery, headquarters company and supply company, would assign one man to work at the canteen after drill hours. For this they received an extra dollar a day from

"My duties really piled up after we arrived at camp. Not only was it expected of me to do regular duty as a first lieutenant in Battery F but the colonel made me regimental canteen officer."

canteen profits. We also had the battery barbers all assigned to the canteen. They charged a quarter for a haircut and a dime for a shave and were allowed to keep 40 percent of what they took in—the rest went to the canteen fund. We also set up a tailor shop where the men could have their uniforms fitted for a small sum. The tailor was also on a percentage basis. All these men had to do military duty as well as work at the canteen.

In order to get started we suggested to the regimental commander that he order each of the battery and head-quarters and supply companies to turn over to the canteen officer from their respective mess funds a sum equal to two dollars per man. There were eleven hundred men in the regiment so Sergeant Jacobson and I had $2,200 as a capital fund with which to start business. After six months' operation we'd paid to the various mess funds $10,000 in dividends and their original investment had been returned. We had a stock on hand of about $5,000. Our overhead was low, our prices were bedrock and we had no credit accounts. The service at our canteen was so good that adjoining regiments were also our patrons. Most canteen officers had trouble with their accounts and got sent home or court martialed. Jacobson and I had good luck—we kept our accounts carefully—insisted on a monthly audit and the canteen officer was recommended for promotion to captain and was sent overseas with the division advance school detail on March 20, 1918.

Three first lieutenants were ordered up for examination for promotion on the same day in February, 1918—Lieutenant Newell T. Paterson of Battery D, Lieutenant Ted Marks of Battery C and Lieutenant Harry S. Truman of Battery F. Paterson went in first—Ted and I had to stay out in the cold (it was about zero or five above) and wait. Paterson stayed an hour and a half and then I was called. When I went into one of the brigade mess halls there sat old General Lucien G. Berry and three Regular Army colonels. General Berry had been the ranking field artillery colonel at the outbreak of the war and had been General Pershing's chief of artillery on his march into Mexico in 1916. He was six feet tall, wore a handlebar mustache and hated National Guard lieutenants. The old man was fond of privates and corporals but took much pleasure in chewing up young officers with his false teeth and spitting them out in small bits—but I'll say this for him, he would not let anyone outside his outfit find fault with his officers or men. Well the general and his three colonels took me over the jumps for about an hour and I came out very sure I'd never be promoted. Then Ted went in. It was getting near lunch time by then so they only kept him thirty minutes. We all got promoted. Paterson's commission was dated April 22, 1918, mine April 23 and Ted's April 24.

Our Colonel Karl D. Klemm and Lieutenant Colonel Arthur J. Elliott had been sent to Houston to a staff officers' school about four weeks before my examination for promotion came up. Lieutenant Colonel Robert M. Danford had been assigned to command the regiment. He had been in command of the Yale Battery and had written a book on field artillery along with Maretti. Danford and Maretti was the last word in firing and battery management.

Colonel (afterward Brigadier General and finally Major General Chief of Field Artillery) Danford was a kind, understanding man. He was a strict disciplinarian but he made all the young officers and the men feel like he wanted to help them become good soldiers and efficient officers. He taught me more about handling men and the fundamentals of artillery fire in six weeks than I'd learned in the six months I'd been going over to the school of fire and attending the regimental schools.

It seemed to be the policy of all high-ranking artillery officers (and I mean from majors up, by high-ranking) to make a deep dark mystery out of the firing of a battery. They taught us logarithms, square root, trigonometry, navigation and logistics but never did tell us that all they wanted to do was to make the projectile hit the target. Danford told us that and most of us were descendants of good old squirrel rifle shots and from then on we did just that—made the shell hit the target. Afterwards when they made me a firing instructor in France, I told the boys right off what we were trying to do and explained at some length that all the trimmings were for was to make the first shot more accurate—after that it was just like any other shooting.

We made some excellent artillerymen out of men who'd never seen an artillery weapon until the war began.

My mother and sister came to see me at Camp Doniphan. My mother was sixty-five years old but she never shed a tear, smiled at me all the time and told me to do my best for the country. But she cried all the way home and when I came back home from France she gained ten or fifteen pounds in weight. That's the real horror of war.

I was ordered overseas with the special school detail of the division. We left Doniphan on March 20 about noon by the Rock Island and arrived in Kansas City at 4:00 A.M. I got a switchman out in the Rosedale yards to let me use his phone and I called my mother and my sweetheart. It was the last time I talked to either for a year and two months.

On March 30, the day before Easter Sunday, we sailed aboard the *George Washington* for France. There we were watching New York's skyline diminish and wondering if we'd be heroes or corpses. Most of us got by without being either. We had an uneventful crossing and landed at Brest on the morning of April 13, 1918. It was a beautiful morning, one of the few we had while over there. They sent the officers to the Continental Hotel and the men to Pontanezen Barracks. We stayed in Brest two or three days and then went to Montigny-sur-Aube to school. Col. Dick Burleson (a Texas Burleson) was in charge. He was a hardboiled gentleman but he knew his artillery and he could impart his knowledge. He taught me to shoot a 75 gun and taught me so well I became able to teach others. We rejoined our regiment on June 8 at Angers where I acted as battalion adjutant for Major Marvin H. Gates of the Second Battalion for one whole month, a most pleasant month, one I'll never forget. Then we moved to Coëtquidan where all the regimental officers except the ones who'd been to Burleson's school went to school again. On the tenth of July the colonel sent for me. I went over everything I'd done for the last ten days to see if I could find out what I was to be bawled out for, but could think of nothing. I waited around in his office until he'd dressed down a second lieutenant or two and then my time came. He suddenly said to me, "Harry, how would you like to command a battery?" "Well, sir," I said, "I hope to be able to do that some day." "All right, you'll take command of D Battery in the morning." I saluted, about-faced and walked out. Then I told the major that my tour of duty in France would be short because Klemm had given me D Battery. They were the wild Irish and German Catholics from Rockhurst Academy in Kansas City. They had had four commanders before me. I wasn't a Catholic, I was a thirty-second degree Mason. I could just see my hide on the fence when I tried to run that outfit.

I've been very badly frightened several times in my life and the morning of July 11, 1918 when I took over that battery was one of those times. I was most anxious to make good in my new rank of captain and I was rather doubtful of my ability to handle that obstreperous battery. For some reason or other we hit it off and they went to the front August 18, 1918, and stayed there until November 11, 1918 under my command and were brought home and discharged May 6, 1919 and all their discharges were signed by me. They took up a collection and bought me a big silver cup with a most beautiful inscription on it and they all continue to call me Captain Harry.

Along in October, notice caught up with me that I was a captain. I'd been in command of Battery D, 129th, since July 11. In May, 1918, I'd seen in the New York *Times* that I was a captain so I wore the bars and did captain's duty but was never paid for it because the official notice did not reach me until October. I put in a claim for the pay and

"I've been very badly frightened several times in my life and the morning of July 11, 1918 when I took over the battery was one of those times."

was turned down. I'd not "accepted" the commission until October—the law's the law q.e.d.

I fired 3,000 rounds of 75 ammunition from 4:00 A.M. to 8:00 A.M., September 26, 1918. I had slept in the edge of a wood to the right of my battery position on Friday night. If I hadn't awaked and got up at 4:00 A.M. I would not be here, because the Germans fired a barrage on my sleeping place! At eight o'clock my battery pulled out for the front. As we marched on a road under an embankment, a French 155-mm. battery fired over my head and I still have trouble hearing what goes on when there is a noise. I went back and told the French captain what I thought of him but he couldn't understand me—so it made no difference.

We came to the front line at a little town, what was left of it, called Boureuilles. I stopped the battery and went forward with my executive officer and the battalion commander, Major Gates. We located a battery of the enemy and sat in a ditch while they fired machine guns over us. Finally went back to the battery and spent the rest of the night getting it across no man's land. At 5:00 A.M., the twenty-seventh of September, the operations officer of the regiment, Major Paterson, came to my sleeping place under a bush and told me to fire a barrage in ten minutes! I told him to go to hell, that I couldn't figure one in ten minutes but I'd try!

Didn't fire a shot but moved up on behind the infantry. Finally went into position on a road between Varennes and Cheppy about 10:00 P.M., September 28. In going into position I rode my horse under a tree and a limb of the tree scraped my glasses off—and I picked them up from the horse's back behind the saddle! No one would believe a tale like that but it happened. I put the battery into position and then moved into an orchard a half mile ahead the next day. Fired on three batteries, destroyed one and put the other two out of business. The regimental colonel threatened me with a court martial for firing out of the Thirty-fifth Division sector! But I saved some men in the Twenty-eighth Division on our left and they were grateful in 1948!

One of my lieutenants was acting as communications officer that afternoon and had a phone set on his head. He looked up and saw a German plane and remarked to the battery exec. that the so-and-so German was dropping something. The bomb went off and cut the phone off his head and didn't hurt him. In the meantime I was up in front of the infantry without a weapon of any kind, observing the enemy fire from every direction. An infantry sergeant came up to my foxhole and told me that my support had moved back 200 yards, and that I'd do well to come back too. I did! . . .

On October 27, 1918, we were moving along the road in France from one front line zone to another when the French edition of the New York *Herald* was distributed along the line. Headlines in black letters informed us that an armistice was on. Just then a German 150 shell burst to the right of the road and another to the left.

One of the sergeants remarked, "Captain, those G.D. Germans haven't seen this paper." On November 7 Roy Howard sent a message to the U.S.A. proclaiming a false armistice. Such false newspaper reports are terrible things and people responsible for them are just one grade below the worst criminal.

We went into new positions on November 6 and prepared barrages for the drive on Metz for November 7. The 129th F.A. was supporting the 81st (Wild Cat) Division.

On November 11, at 5:00 A.M., Major Paterson, the regimental operations officer, called me and told me that there would be a cease-fire order at 11:00 A.M.—that was November 11, 1918. I fired the battery on orders until 10:45 when I fired my last shot on a little village—Hermeville—

northeast of Verdun. The last range was 11,000 meters with the new D shell. Eighty-eight hundred meters was the extreme range of the 75-mm. gun with regular ammunition, but with the streamlined D shell it would reach 11,500 meters.

We stopped firing all along the line at eleven o'clock, November 11, 1918. It was so quiet it made your head ache. We stayed at our positions all day and then crawled into our pup tents that evening.

There was a French battery of old Napoleon six-inch guns just behind my battery position. These old Napoleon guns had wheels six feet in diameter and no recoil mechanism. They'd run back up tall wooden contraptions built like a carpenter's sawhorse and then run down into place again. If a gunner got in the way either going or coming he'd lose an arm or a leg or any other part of his anatomy that happened to be in the way of the old gun. It was a good gun, though, and would hit the target if laid by an expert.

Along in the evening all the men in the French battery became intoxicated as a result of a load of wine which came up on the ammunition narrow gauge. Every single one of them had to march by my bed and salute and yell, "Vive President Wilson, Vive le capitaine d'artillerie américaine!" No sleep all night, the infantry fired Very pistols, sent up all the flares they could lay their hands on, fired rifles, pistols and whatever else would make noise, all night long.

Next day we had orders to leave our guns in line and fall back to the echelon. After that we spent our evenings playing poker and wishing we were at home.

On December 7 a number of officers were given a leave. I was one of them. We went to Paris where we spent three happy days. I attended "Manon" at the Comedie Française. Went to the Opéra Comique to hear "Carmen," and to the Folies Bergères, a disgusting performance. Then we went to Nice, stayed at the Hotel Méditerranée, saw the American Bar in the Hotel Negresco and the one in the Rue des Anglais, visited the Casino at Monte Carlo, but we couldn't play because we were in uniform.

They gave us a five-franc chip and that's all we had from the famous gambling hell.

We had lunch one day in the Casino de Paris. There were about seven or eight of us sitting at a big round table in the rear of the place, when all of a sudden every waiter in the place rushed to the front and began bowing and scraping, and we were informed that Madame la Princesse de Monaco had come in. Our lieutenant colonel was facing the front and could see the performance. He watched very closely and pretty soon he reported, "Oh, hell, she's taking beer! Can you imagine a princess drinking beer?" It gave all of us common people a letdown.

We went back to the regiment, moved a couple of times, and finally landed back in Brest where we took off for U.S.A. on April 9, 1919, landing in New York on Sunday—Easter Sunday morning, April 20. I'd been gone from that city just a year and twenty days. I made a resolution that if old lady Liberty in New York harbor wanted to see me again she'd have to turn around.

We were sent to Camp Mills and then ordered to Camp Funston, Kansas, for discharge. The discharge was accomplished on May 6, 1919.

CHAPTER V

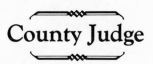

County Judge

After my discharge I went back to the farm and on June 28, 1919 my wedding to Miss Bess Wallace took place—the same beautiful, blue-eyed, golden hair girl referred to earlier in this manuscript.

The farm in the meantime had been broken up. My maternal grandmother had left it to my uncle, for whom I was named, and my mother. The uncle lived with us until he passed away, which happened while I was away at war. He left his part of the farm to be divided into four parts— one to my mother and the other three parts to my brother, my sister and myself. When my grandmother died there was a will contest and a settlement which placed a back-breaking mortgage of about $30,000 on the farm. When my uncle died, and the property was divided, my mother's part still had to carry a very large part of this mortgage. Accumulated interest and other difficulties had by 1934 increased the charge to about $35,000; although I'd sold some of the land, which my mother and I held together, and had paid some twelve or fifteen thousand dollars on the indebtedness it still continued to pile up. Very bad years, both wet and dry, added to the difficulty so that interest and overhead kept the debt right around $35,000.

My canteen sergeant being a furnishing goods man wanted to open a store on Twelfth Street in Kansas City so I established a line of credit with a couple of banks and we opened a men's furnishing store at 104 West Twelfth along late in 1919. A flourishing business was carried on for about a year and a half and then came the squeeze of 1921. Jacobson and I went to bed one night with a $35,000 inventory and awoke the next day with a $25,000 shrinkage. As Mark Twain said about his watch, this brought bills payable and bank notes due at such a rapid rate we went out of business. All the bank notes were paid off and the merchandise bills were settled as equitably as could be managed. It took several years to clean everything up. The store was finally closed up along in the latter part of 1922. Early in March, 1922, the Democrats began talking about candidates for county judge for the eastern district of Jackson County. The eastern district is all that part of the county outside the city limits of Kansas City.

I had sold my stock and farm equipment early in 1921 and used the money in trying to meet the situation at the store. My wife and I had been living at Independence with her mother. Mr. William Southern, editor and publisher of the Independence *Examiner*, the most widely read paper in Jackson County outside Kansas City, suggested to some of the eastern Jackson County politicians that if they wanted a candidate for eastern judge who could win they should take an ex-soldier of the late war. He suggested Harry Truman. I knew nothing of this until a delegation of men from the county came into my store on Twelfth Street and asked me to run.

My father having been road overseer, and both of us having always been interested in politics to some extent, I knew all the men in the delegation personally. They told me about Mr. Southern's suggestion to the "Goat" faction of the Democrats and urged me to go. The Democrats in eastern Jackson County had always to some extent been aligned with the two factions in Kansas City. The "Goats" were with the Pendergast faction and the "Rabbits" were with Shannon. My friends told me that the presiding judge of the county court, Miles Bulger, expected to have a candidate of his own because he'd fallen out with Tom Pendergast and that Joe Shannon would support E.E. Montgomery, a banker at Blue Springs. They also told me that George Shaw, a former road contractor and a fine old man, and James Compton then serving out a term as eastern judge by appointment of the governor, would be independent candidates. They told me that the eastern Jackson

County "Goat" faction would back me tooth and nail and that if I won the nomination the "Rabbits" had agreed to support me.

Well, the store was closing up—I liked the political game and I knew personally half the people in eastern Jackson County. I also had kinfolks in nearly every precinct and I decided to make the race. It was a hot affair. I opened my campaign in Lee's Summit with Colonel (now Major General) E.M. Stayton making the principal address. The colonel had been in command of the 110th Engineers in the 35th Division. He knew my war record, what there was of it, and he made the most of it. From June 1 to August 5, 1922, I made every township and precinct in the county and when the votes were counted on the first Tuesday in August, I had a plurality of 500 votes.

The election in the fall went off without incident because eastern Jackson County is as Democratic as Mississippi or South Carolina. I was sworn in on January 1, 1923 and went to work trying to learn everything I could about the law and the duties attached to my new job. I had an old Dodge roadster, the roughest riding car ever built, but sturdy enough to take the gullies and mudholes of every crossroads in the county. Every road, bridge, lane and every county institution was thoroughly examined. County court procedure was studied in every detail. All this was useful some years afterward.

The new court was made up of a fine old gentleman by the name of Elihu Hayes who was the presiding judge and H.F. McElroy, who was judge for the western district or Kansas City. Judge McElroy had a newspaper complex— he was very friendly to the Kansas City *Star* and was known as the *Star*'s man on the court. He was also a close friend of T.J. Pendergast. In fact he introduced me to T.J. Pendergast the first time I ever saw him.

"The election in the fall went off without incident because eastern Jackson County is as Democratic as Mississippi or South Carolina. I was sworn in on January 1, 1923 . . ." [Judge-elect Truman, beaming.]

The court was almost always in a fuss about something. Hayes representing the "Rabbits" wanted certain jobs in county institutions and as road overseers and McElroy wanted usually the same jobs for the "Goats." Public service was a secondary matter if the political factions could get the jobs they wanted. I acted as a sort of an arbitrator and finally got Hayes, McElroy and Tom and Joe to sit down and reach an agreement so we could get the jobs out of the way and do a little work for the taxpayers. It was an uphill job. By 1924 the factions were so widely split that McElroy and I were beaten for re-election. During 1925 and the early part of 1926 I put on a whirlwind membership campaign for the Kansas City Automobile Club and made a good living at it.

When the politicians met early in 1926 to decide on procedure for the fall campaign I went to see Mike Pendergast and told him I'd like to run for county collector. It was a good job at that time and paid a return to the collector of about $25,000 per year. I figured I could make a record collecting back taxes and could also pay all my accumulated debts and maybe go back to the farm at the end of eight years and enjoy life. Mike Pendergast was young Jim's father who was my personal friend. He was anxious for me to have what I wanted—but it didn't happen.

T.J. and his advisers (and he had a very competent staff of advisers at that time) decided that since I was familiar with the county court business I'd be a better public servant as presiding judge of the county court. Besides that an older man and one who had been with the organization longer was entitled to be county collector. I filed for presiding judge, much to the disgust of Mike Pendergast who wanted me to make a fight for collector.

There was no opposition in the primary and my majority in the fall election was a little over 16,000 votes. In the spring of 1926 Kansas City had adopted a new charter, which created a city manager form of government. The Democrats won five of the nine aldermen and they elected Judge McElroy as city manager. He made an excellent city manager for more than eight years and then the scandals came and he died just a short time before Tom Pendergast was convicted of income tax evasion.

I set to work as presiding judge to clean up the county's financial condition. The number of employees was reduced, the road overseers cut down from sixty to sixteen, a budget system installed, outstanding county warrants were called in and refinanced on a low interest basis and plans were prepared for a county road and public building program.

It was the common procedure under the law for the county to sell notes anticipating tax collections. Tax collections did not start until September so the county had to issue notes against anticipated revenue and sell them to the banks for money to transact the county's business. The law stated that these notes should bear interest not to exceed 6 percent—and the banks always charged 6 percent.

These notes were absolutely gilt edge, because they could not be issued in an amount exceeding 90 percent of the anticipated revenue, and the court's judgment and finding on the anticipated revenue was based on a five-year average. The anticipated revenue was always below what was actually collected. So the county instead of paying 6 percent should have had the same rate the state and federal government had to pay for bonds. I took it on myself to interview the three big banks in the town and they treated me like I was trying to steal something from their stockholders. My attitude was that the taxpayers had some rights in the matter too, so a trip was made to Chicago and St. Louis and communications were sent to Eastern bankers and the next tax notes sold for 4-1/2 percent.

The rate kept going down until along toward the end of my second term as presiding judge the rate was as low as 1-1/2 percent. It never did go up to 6 percent again.

In 1928 Kansas City on the advice of a committee of one hundred of the leading businessmen, labor leaders and professional men decided to make a major plan for civic improvements. This plan included a new city hall, civic auditorium, water works plant and traffic entrances to the city.

The county court had made some surveys for a road system and had need for a new court house in Kansas City and a remodeling of the one at Independence. A hospital was also badly needed at the county home for the aged. It was my job to try and get the county's bond plan included at the same election at which the city's would be voted upon. The political leaders—T.J. Pendergast and Joseph B. Shannon—were interviewed, as well as the committee of one hundred, the chambers of commerce of both cities, and the county leaders in the various towns and townships.

The political leaders did not think a bond issue for the county would carry—two such proposed issues had been defeated about ten years previously when Miles Bulger was presiding judge. The county court, however, were of the opinion that the bond issue for the county could be put over. We appointed a bipartisan board of engineers to draw up a complete road plan for the county and two leading firms of architects of the city and a consulting architect from Shreveport, Louisiana were appointed to make preliminary plans for the public buildings. The engineers were Colonel E.M. Stayton and N.T. Veatch, Jr., the architects were Keene and Simpson and Wight and Wight with Edward Neild as consultant. I told the politicians and the two political leaders in particular that if I could go to the voters and assure them that these able engineers and

61

"I had an old Dodge roadster, the roughest riding car ever built, but sturdy enough to take the gullies and mudholes of every crossroads in the county."

architects would have control of the construction and that no payments would be made by the court without their approval, I thought the bonds would carry. Pendergast and Shannon told me to tell the voters anything I pleased. I made it perfectly plain to both of them that I intended to carry out the promise if the bonds carried.

The bonds did carry and the program was carried out to the letter. The presiding judge had visited a dozen or more new public buildings, court houses, city halls and state capitols. The court house at Shreveport seemed most satisfactory so its architect, Mr. Edward Neild, was employed as consultant. The presiding judge also visited Cook County, Illinois, Wayne County, Michigan, Westchester County, New York and a number of other counties and examined their road systems. It is generally conceded that Jackson County, Missouri came out with a good road system and a good set of public buildings.

When the election of 1930 came up we were in the midst of the building and budget reform programs so the presiding judge and associate judges favorable to the policy being pursued were returned to office. The majority of the presiding judge was over 58,000 votes. It was in fact a vote of confidence.

In 1932 a reapportionment of representatives to the national congress caused a loss of three House members to Missouri. The legislature could not agree on a redistricting of the state so the thirteen House members were elected by the state at large. In the 1933 session of the state legislature, however, the state was redistricted and Jackson County obtained two districts from which to elect House members. The Fourth District is all that part of the county outside Kansas City except Washington Township, which lies south of the city and three or four of the east side city wards. The Fifth District is all the city except the wards in the Fourth and Washington Township.

I helped arrange the Fourth District because my ambition was to become a member of the House of Representatives. I believed I could go to the House from the new Fourth District and stay as long as I chose to stay but when the party caucus was held to decide on candidates in the 1934 election from Jackson my good friend Judge C. Jasper Bell had talked T.J. Pendergast into endorsing him for congressman from the Fourth District and my plan to be a congressman went out the window. I decided to go back to the farm and stay out of politics but that didn't happen either.

In 1932 the Kansas City Democratic organization (Pendergast and Shannon) endorsed Charles M. Howell for United States senator. Bennett Champ Clark was the other candidate. When the votes were counted in the August primary that year Mr. Howell had 110,000 votes in Kansas City and Jackson County and had carried about three other counties. Clark carried all the rest of the state and was overwhelmingly nominated and was elected that fall.

In the spring of 1934 Missouri was voting on a bond issue to enlarge the various eleemosynary institutions—four or five insane hospitals and the penitentiary. Governor Park asked me to make some speeches out over the state and help make the bond campaign a success. I am a member of the American Legion, Veterans of Foreign Wars, was in the line of the Masonic grand lodge and was very active in the county judges association, which was made up of the county judges in 114 counties. The governor thought perhaps I could be helpful. We made up a bipartisan team and went into thirty-five counties. I don't know whether we helped or not but the bond issue won.

CHAPTER VI

Senator

Along in the first week in May [1934] I was speaking in Warsaw, Missouri on the bond issue when I received a phone call from Sedalia, which is about thirty miles from Warsaw, asking me to stop at the Bothwell Hotel on my way north and have a talk with James P. Aylward, the state chairman of the Democratic committee and Jim Pendergast, nephew of T.J. and my war buddy. I stopped and talked to them and they urged me to run for the nomination to the United States Senate. I told them that I had no legislative experience, that I thought I was something of an executive and I'd rather wait two years and run for governor. But they insisted that I owed it to the party to run, that Senator Clark was from the eastern side of the state and that Jackson County was entitled to one of the senators. Aylward assured me he could line up his friends in St. Louis and that I'd have no trouble beating Tuck Milligan, who was congressman from the Third District and who had been endorsed by Senator Clark. Well after some argument back and forth I went to Jefferson City and filed for the Senate. Mr. Aylward couldn't do any good in St. Louis. The Democratic organization down there had a candidate of their own, Congressman John J. Cochran.

It was a tough three-cornered race. When the smoke blew away, I was nominated by some 40,000 plurality. I got the votes in Jackson County. Cochran got those in St. Louis and St. Louis County and Milligan, Cochran and I split the country vote. I carried forty counties outside Jackson and ran second in sixty. My wide acquaintance in the state and particularly my association with county judges and county clerks is the answer to my being able to win with the support of the Kansas City organization, while Charles M. Howell, former state chairman of the Democratic committee, widely known lawyer and insurance

67

man, could not win. I made a very strenuous campaign, covering practically the whole state outside St. Louis, and I think showed that people would vote for me.

The election in the fall of 1934 was a pushover for the Democrats so I came to the United States Senate and went to work. I was in luck on committee assignments: Interstate Commerce, Appropriations, and a couple of minor ones—Printing, and Public Buildings and Grounds. Senator Wheeler was chairman of Interstate Commerce and Senator Glass was chairman of Appropriations. Wheeler had succeeded in getting a resolution through the Senate authorizing the Interstate Commerce Committee or any subcommittee thereof to investigate the financial transactions of the railroads. That subcommittee, of which Wheeler appointed himself chairman, began its deliberations along in the fall of 1935. Being interested in transportation and communications I attended the meetings of the subcommittee. Wheeler saw that I was interested and finally made me one of the subcommittee members and later its vice chairman. Sitting as a "hearing committee" is a dull, boresome procedure and it requires patience and persistence, so I soon became the "patient and persistent" member of the subcommittee of the Interstate Commerce Committee on railroad finance. The work of that subcommittee finally resulted in the Wheeler-Truman Bill—the Transportation Act of 1940. That bill was introduced in 1938 by Senator Wheeler for himself and the junior senator from Missouri and after two years of hard work on it and three years of hearings on railroad finance methods, it became law. I learned much about procedure in the Senate, about New York banker and lawyer methods and how the House and Senate came to conclusions on legislation during this time. Senator Glass had placed me upon most of the important subcommittees of the Appropriations Committee also and I sat on many hearings for funds

"The election in the fall of 1934 was a pushover for the Democrats so I came to the United States Senate and went to work." [Truman taking oath as senator, 1935.]

and many conference committees of the two houses of Congress.

During my first term as senator I was chairman of the subcommittee of the Interstate Commerce Committee out of which came the Civil Aeronautics Act. Senator Donahey of Ohio was appointed chairman of that sub-committee but did not attend the meetings. Senator Austin of Vermont and I carried on the hearings over a couple of years and finally presented a bill to the Senate which became the Civil Aeronautics Act.

Senator Clark having come to the Senate in 1933 a few days before the Democratic administration took over had succeeded in filling all federal patronage appointments before I arrived. Both district attorneys were recommended by him as were U.S. marshals and collectors of revenue for the eastern and the western districts of Missouri. None of these gentlemen were in sympathy either with me or the policies of the Roosevelt administration—Senator Clark having taken at the beginning of the Roosevelt term a stand with the opposition—so when the terms of the district attorney and U.S. marshal came to an end in 1937 I recommended other men for their places. But the vote fraud scandals and Pendergast troubles were rife about that time and the administration didn't have the nerve to back up its friends in Missouri.

In 1936 Missouri had reelected a whole Democratic state ticket except the governor who by constitutional provision could not succeed himself. A nursery man by the name of Lloyd Stark from Louisiana, Missouri was elected governor. He graduated from Annapolis along in 1904 or 1905 and served a few years in the navy and then went back to the nursery at Louisiana. When World War I came along he joined the army and became a major of field artillery. After the war was over he became interested in civic and Legion affairs and became well known over the state. He wanted to be a candidate for governor in 1932 but Francis Wilson, a resident of Platte County who had been defeated in 1928 in the Hoover-Al Smith fiasco, was renominated. Before the election some time along in the fall he suddenly passed away and it was up to the state committee of the Democratic party to nominate a man.

Jackson County was putting on a grand celebration at Sni-a-Bar Farms on the day Wilson died, commemorating the completion of the road and public building program. It was the biggest barbecue and picnic ever held in western Missouri—some thirty-five thousand people attended. It was my big day. After the celebration was over I went to Excelsior Springs and stayed a couple of days. The state committee met in Kansas City the day after Wilson's death and nominated Guy B. Park of Platte County. He was a judge of the Missouri circuit court and a very fine gentleman. He made a good governor, and that in spite of violent newspaper opposition. Lloyd Stark had wanted the state committee to make him the candidate and he was sorely disappointed when they didn't.

After I was elected to the Senate in 1934 I had many political contacts and personal ones also in nearly every county in the state. Along in February, 1935, Lloyd Stark called me from his home in Louisiana, Missouri and informed me that he had a boy at Annapolis Naval Academy, that he was leaving home on a certain day to go and see the boy and that he would like very much to see me on the same trip. Of course, I told him to stop in Washington on his way over to Annapolis or on the way back home from there and I'd be glad to see and talk to him as long as he liked. Mr. Stark had been one of my supporters in the bitter 1934 primary fight in Missouri and I felt friendly and grateful to him.

He came in to see me sometime in February, 1935. His mission was to tell me that he wanted to be governor of

Missouri and that he knew he couldn't make the grade unless he had the support of the Democratic organization in Kansas City and he wanted me to tell him how to get T.J. Pendergast to be for him. I gave him the names of the leaders in sixty or seventy of the counties in Missouri who were my personal and political friends and suggested to him that he see them and have them write or call on Pendergast and tell him that they believed that Lloyd Stark would poll more votes in 1936 than anyone else in 1936 for governor. Evidently he saw most of them. Along in July he came to my office again. He had been there once or twice a month since February—but in July he had another ax to grind in his ambition to be governor of Missouri. He told me that he'd seen Bennett Clark and that Bennett had agreed to go to New York to see Tom Pendergast in his behalf if I would go along. Tom had returned from one of his numerous trips to Europe on the big transatlantic liners—the *Roma* or *Queen Mary* or the *Normandie*—and was at the Waldorf-Astoria.

I called Senator Clark and he confirmed the statement of Mr. Stark. Then I called Pendergast and told him that Clark and I would like to see him in New York the next day. He couldn't do anything else but see us. Two United States senators can see anyone—no matter who—and T.J. was first of all a good politician. He was, as always with me, very cordial and said he would be most happy to see Bennett and me. We saw him the next day in the Waldorf and Bennett told him that this man Stark had no political experience, that he was an egotist and not to be depended upon. I told Tom that I thought Stark was an honorable man and that he would make a good governor, which shows how easy it is to be fooled by your friends. Stark had neither honor nor loyalty. He should have been a member of the Spanish Inquisition or of the Court of

Louis XI of France. Some day when I have time I'll write a character sketch of him that will be very interesting.

When the interview was over Pendergast called me aside and told me to tell Stark on the way back to Washington that if he would bring some good old country Democrat to Kansas City along in October (1935) and discuss his ambitions that he (Pendergast) would publicly announce for him for governor. On the way back to Washington I told Stark what Pendergast had said to me. I almost had to leave the drawing room to prevent his hugging and kissing me. He appeared to be the most grateful man alive and told me that he'd do anything any time to help me.

He was elected governor in 1936. Took office on January 8, 1937. Came to see me as U.S. senator just once after that. When he'd come to Washington as governor of Missouri he'd call on the president, the vice president, the secretary of war or navy and go out of town. On one occasion when he was calling on the vice president he stuck his head into the door of my reception room and told my secretary that certain rumors were about that he (Stark) was a candidate for the Senate in 1940. He assured my secretary that there was no truth in these rumors. I told the secretary that I'd bet my last dollar that Mr. Stark would try for my place in 1940.

He did and so did the district attorney whose appointment I'd opposed on the grounds of inefficiency. The D.A. resigned on account of the Hatch Act and made a bitter and vicious campaign against me. Stark had denounced Pendergast and had the support of all the metropolitan newspapers. It looked very dark for the junior senator from Missouri but he stayed by his friends and when the smoke cleared away and the votes were counted he was still the junior senator from Missouri. People like public servants who serve them and they like friendship and loyalty to friends. Friends don't count in fair weather. It is when trouble comes that friends count.

I was nominated by a plurality of 8,400 votes in the August primary, after the most bitter, mud-slinging campaign in Missouri's history of dirty campaigns. At eleven o'clock on the night of the primary vote I went to bed eleven thousand votes behind and supposedly defeated. The Kansas City *Star* and the St. Louis *Post-Dispatch* had extras out telling how happy they were and safe Missouri was from my slimy person as senator. A lying press cannot fool the people. I came back to the Senate and the double-crossing ingrate of a governor was sent back to the nursery.

The district attorney Mr. Milligan had turned on all the power of his office to try to find something wrong with my record as a public official. Of course he couldn't find it but he made the same bitter campaign as if he had found it. The violently partisan Republican federal judge at Kansas City finally had to tell him to stick to facts.

I started my second term as junior senator from Missouri on January 3, 1941. After the election and in between I'd been working on military and naval appropriations. In 1939 I had made a trip with the Military Subcommittee of the Appropriations Committee to all the defense points in the United States and in Panama, Central America, Cuba and Puerto Rico. This was after Hitler went into Poland. Our situation was shocking. *We had no defenses.* In 1940 was passed a Universal Service Law. I had been in the National Guard of Missouri from 1905 to 1917, in the First World War from 1917 to 1919, and an officer in the field artillery reserve from 1919 to 1940. I had been training reserve officers at camps and in night schools from 1920 to 1940, so I went down to see the Chief of Staff, General Marshall, and told him I'd like to quit the Senate and go into service as a field artillery colonel and an instructor in

F.A. tactics. He asked how old I was and I told him I was fifty-six years old. He pulled his reading glasses down on his nose, grinned at me and said, "We don't need old stiffs like you—this will be a young man's war." He was right, of course, but it hurt my feelings and I decided to do something for the war effort on a constructive basis.

After we had appropriated about twenty-five billions of dollars for national defense I took my old coupe and began inspecting camp construction and naval installations from Maine to Florida and from Pennsylvania to New Mexico, California, Washington and along both borders north and south. Some 30,000 miles were covered. This while the bitter Missouri election campaign was on also.

On February 18, 1941 I made a statement to the Senate on what I'd seen, and asked that a special committee be authorized to look into defense expenditures. I believe that statement resulted in the saving of billions of the taxpayers' money and thousands of lives of our fighting men.

A great deal of difficulty was experienced in getting the Committee on Audit and Control to authorize funds after the Military Affairs Committee had decided that a special committee to investigate the national defense program ought to be authorized. James F. Byrnes was chairman of the Committee on Audit and Control. He is a very cagey politician and he was afraid that the junior senator from Missouri wanted a political weapon, although he'd just been returned to the Senate for another six years and could afford to be a statesman for at least four years. Mr. Byrnes finally agreed to give the committee the munificent sum of $15,000 to investigate the expenditure of $25 billion. The vice president appointed the committee of seven senators with Truman as chairman and we went to work.

The committee was made up of five Democrats and two Republicans. If my memory is not at fault Senators Connally, Hayden, Wallgren, Mead and Truman were the majority members and Senators Ball and Brewster the minority. Senator Hayden couldn't serve because of his duties on the Appropriations Committee and chairman of the Joint Committee on Printing.

The first problem was the selection of a committee counsel. Senator Connally had a good friend in Texas whom he wanted appointed—a Mr. Hill, a very fine gentleman who afterwards became an assistant secretary of agriculture. The chairman of the Special Committee, however, had some ideas on the subject of a counselor and before making a decision, having had some administrative experience in presiding over the county court in Jackson County, I knew what a vital part of the administrative procedure a counselor could be. So I made a trip down the Avenue to see the attorney general, who at that time was the Honorable Robert H. Jackson. He is a great man—was a great attorney general and has made an able justice of the Supreme Court. I told the attorney general that I wanted a counselor for the new Special Committee to Investigate the National Defense Program; that I wanted an able lawyer, one who knew a fact when he saw one and that I wanted him to be able to prosecute a case to its conclusion, if prosecution became necessary, without being a persecutor. I also specified that I didn't want a man with a publicity complex. I wanted him to get the facts, question witnesses and advise the committee, but that policy would be decided by the committee itself. Jackson told me that such a man was impossible to find but he would try to get me one.

Mr. Hugh Fulton was recommended by Attorney General Jackson, was employed by the committee, and met the specifications. From first to last he did a real job. So with a good counselor and seven senators who wanted results in the war effort we had excellent results. We made no statements unless we had the facts. We

"On February 18, 1941 I made a statement to the Senate on [national defense] and asked that a special committee be authorized to look into defense expenditures. I believe that statement resulted in the saving of billions of the taxpayers' money and thousands of lives of our fighting men." [The Senate Special Committee to Investigate the National Defense Program, of which Truman was chairman.]

wanted no one smeared or whitewashed and after two years of very hard work the committee had a national reputation for energy and integrity.

We saw the seamy side of the war effort. We had to investigate crooked contractors on camp construction, airplane engine manufacturers who made faulty ones, steel plate factories which cheated, and hundreds of other such sordid and unpatriotic ventures. We investigated procurement, labor hoarding, army and navy waste in food and other supplies. But when we were coming to our conclusions, we all decided that by and large the greatest production and war preparation job in history had been done.

We looked into rubber and made a report on it in May, 1941, which resulted in the Baruch plan. We found cartel agreements by the great oil and aluminum companies which were helpful to the enemy, and we found labor leaders who were willing to sacrifice the country for their own aggrandizement. Publicity is the best antidote for this sort of thing and the committee acted as a sounding board to the country. We made some thirty reports over a three-year period and due to the painstaking care with which facts were assembled and presented not one report contained minority views.

CHAPTER VII

My Relationship with T. J. Pendergast

There has been much speculation about my relationship politically with T. J. Pendergast (Tom). He became a powerful political boss in Missouri after 1926. His career ended in the early 1940s. . . .

In Battery B at Camp Doniphan was a young man by the name of James M. Pendergast, son of Michael J. Pendergast, older brother of T. J. Pendergast.

I became very well acquainted with young Jim during the war. . . .

Along in July or August 1921, Jim Pendergast brought his father M. J. to see me at the little store Eddie Jacobson and I were operating on West Twelfth Street in Kansas City.

Mike Pendergast was head of the "Goat" organization in the old Tenth Ward of Kansas City and was recognized in the country part of Jackson County as the head of the Pendergast organization outside Kansas City.

M. J. asked me if I would consider the nomination to the county court from the eastern district. I told him I would. . . .

Well, to make it short, I filed for eastern judge at the proper time in 1922. . . . When it came time for re-election in 1924 the "Rabbits" bolted the ticket because of differences over patronage and I was defeated by a nice old Republican harnessmaker in Independence, who afterwards became locally famous for that feat.

I went to work after my defeat but kept up my political contacts. In 1926 the factions patched up their difference. In the spring, Kansas City adopted a new city manager style charter and the Democrats elected five of the nine councilmen and appointed Henry McElroy city manager. He had been my colleague on the county court from the western district which was Kansas City.

I was nominated and elected presiding judge of the county court in the fall election and took office January 1, 1927.

Then I had my first contacts with T. J. Pendergast and Joseph B. Shannon. They were interested in county patronage and also in county purchases. The court appointed the purchasing agent, a county welfare officer, a county auditor, heads of homes, approved the budgets of elected officials of the county, such as treasurer, county clerk, circuit clerk, county collector, county assessor, county highway engineer. The court also appointed road overseers and various other officials. There were about nine hundred patronage jobs and they could be the foundation of a political organization.

T. J. Pendergast was interested in having as many friends in key positions as possible but he always took the position that if a man didn't do the job he was supposed to do, fire him and get someone who would. I always followed that policy.

When the court was ready to let the first road contracts Mr. Pendergast called me and told me that he was in trouble with the local road contractors and would I meet and talk with them. I told him I would. I met them with T. J. P. present. They gave me the old song and dance about being local citizens and taxpayers and that they should have an inside track to the construction contracts.

I told them that the contracts would be let to the lowest bidders wherever they came from and that the specifications would be adhered to strictly. T. J. turned to his friends and said, "I told you that he's the contrariest man in the county. Get out of here." When they were gone he said to me, "You carry out your commitments to the voters." I did just that. But there was a three-man court and the two bosses, Pendergast and Shannon, could have ruined me if they'd wanted to. Tom Pendergast was a man of his word and he kept it with me. My handling of the county business became an asset to the Democratic organization. . . .

T. J. Pendergast never talked to me about my duties as county judge except in matters of patronage—but the one time on the bond issue contracts and then he supported me. He only talked to me once about my work in the Senate and that was when Senator Alben Barkley was running for floor leader. Jim Farley called Mr. Pendergast and asked him to call me and "tell" me to support Barkley. Well, he called me from Colorado Springs and I told him that I was pledged to Pat Harrison of Mississippi because Pat had asked me to vote for him and that Pat had made some speeches for me in the Missouri campaign, and that I'd stand by Senator Harrison. T. J. said, "I told Jim that if you were committed you'd stand by your commitment, because you are a contrary Missourian." I voted for Pat and told Barkley in advance that I would. When Barkley was elected I supported him loyally.

On no other occasion did T. J. Pendergast ever talk to me about my actions in the Senate. He was an able, clear thinker and understood political situations and how to handle them better than any man I have ever known. His word was better than the contracts of most men and he never forgot his verbal commitments. His physical breakdown in 1936 caused all his trouble.

I never deserted him when he needed friends. Many for whom he'd done much more than he ever did for me ran out on him when the going was rough. I didn't do that— and I am president of the United States in my own right!

Because Pendergast was persecuted over his financial difficulties and was convicted of income tax fraud and went to federal prison at Leavenworth, he has been used by people opposed to me in an effort to discredit me. The opposition people whether in the Democratic Party in

"T. J. Pendergast . . . was an able, clear thinker and understood political situations and how to handle them better than any man I have ever known. His physical breakdown in 1936 caused all his trouble." [Harry S. Truman, Thomas J. Pendergast, James P. Aylward, N. G. Robertson, James A. Farley and David A. Fitzgerald at the Democratic National Convention in Philadelphia, 1936.]

1940 or in the sabotage press or the lying columnists or the poor old wrecked Republican Party and its present-day character assassination methods have never been able to hurt me politically by slander and abuse. They never will.

After I was through in the county at home, several grand juries, both state and federal, went over my career as a county judge with a fine tooth comb and they could only give me a clean bill of health. That's the answer.

CHAPTER VIII

Nomination for Vice President

D ue to the fact that the chairman was in charge, presided most of the time at the meetings of the [Truman] committee, he naturally was most often mentioned in connection with the hearings and findings of the committee.

When the 1944 election was approaching mention began to be made about Truman for vice president. Every effort was made by me to shut it off. I liked my job as a senator and I wanted to stay with it. It takes a long time for a man to establish himself in the Senate. I was a member of three very important standing committees—Appropriations, Interstate Commerce, and Military Affairs—and was well up on the list on all of them for seniority, which is very important. My Special Committee was doing good work and I wanted to stay with it.

Several senators who were up for re-election wanted me to go to their states and say a good word for them. I did go to Florida, Utah, California and Arizona on that sort of a mission and wrote some letters for other senators. I do not know whether statements from me helped any or not but the senators seemed to think they did.

When convention time came along I was made a delegate-at-large from Missouri and assigned to the national platform committee on which I'd served in 1936 and 1940.

I had tried to make it very plain wherever I went that I was not a candidate for vice president. While it is a very high office and one of honor, I did not want it. I liked my job as senator from Missouri, and since I couldn't get into the armed forces, as I wanted to, I felt I was making a contribution to the war effort as chairman of the Special Committee and as member of the Military Affairs Committee and the Military Subcommittee on Appropriations.

There were two dozen men at the Chicago convention of the Democrats in 1944 who would have gladly taken the

87

honor of the vice presidential nomination and have been exceedingly happy with it. I spent a most miserable week in trying to stave off the nomination.

As I was about to leave the house in Independence for the Chicago convention of the Democratic Party, the telephone rang. It was Jimmy Byrnes in Washington. He told me that President Roosevelt had decided on him for vice president—that is, the new nominee for vice president at the Chicago convention.

Wallace was not popular as vice president either in the Senate or with the politicians who ran things in the party organization. So when Byrnes called and told me that the president had decided to have him as his running mate for the fourth term I just took it for granted that things were fixed.

Byrnes asked me to nominate him. I told him I'd be glad to do it if the president wanted him.

As I started for the car again to go to Chicago I was called back to the telephone. It was Alben Barkley, majority leader of the Senate. He asked me to nominate him for vice president in the convention. I told him that Byrnes had just called me and told me that the president had decided on him for the place and had asked me to nominate him, and that I'd agreed to do it.

When I arrived in Chicago I had breakfast with Sidney Hillman who was a power in the labor section of the convention. I asked him if he would support Byrnes. He said he would not—that there were only two men he would support. They were William O. Douglas, justice of the Supreme Court, and Harry S. Truman, U.S. senator from Missouri.

I told him that I was not a candidate and that I had agreed to nominate Byrnes because he told me the president wanted him.

Then I had a meeting with Phil Murray, head of the C.I.O., and one with Whitney, head of the Railroad Trainmen. Both told me exactly what Sidney Hillman had told me.

The next morning William Green, head of the A.F. of L., asked me to breakfast at the Palmer House. He told me that the A.F. of L. did not like Wallace and that they had decided to support me. I told him my position with Byrnes and that I was not a candidate.

While we were talking Senators Tydings and George Radcliffe came over to our table and asked me to come over to their table and shake hands with the Maryland delegation to the convention. I went over thinking perhaps I could drum up some support for Byrnes.

Tydings introduced me as the Maryland candidate for vice president! I explained my situation and went back to finish my conversation with Mr. Green.

I reported all these conversations to Byrnes just as they happened. He would tell me every time I'd report just to wait—the president would straighten everybody out in plenty of time.

On Tuesday evening Bob Hannegan came to see me and told me that President Roosevelt wanted me to run with him on the ticket for vice president. This astonished me greatly. Hannegan showed me a longhand note in the president's handwriting which said, "Bob, it's Truman. FDR."

It was written on a scratch pad from the president's desk.

I told Bob that I was not a candidate and that I was committed to Byrnes who had told me that the president was for him.

The president had written a letter in which he had said he would be satisfied with Wallace or Douglas and he had made a public statement in which he said if he were in the convention as a delegate he would vote for Wallace.

Later when he came to Chicago on his way to San Diego, California, he had dictated another note to Hannegan and Ed Pauley in which he said he would be satisfied with either me or Douglas.

I reported all this to Byrnes and he still told me that the president wanted him.

On Thursday before the vice president was to be nominated Hannegan called me and asked me to come over to the Blackstone Hotel to a meeting of the Democratic leaders. I went. Ed Flynn, New York, Mayor Kelly, Chicago, Mayor Hague, Jersey City, George Allen, Ed Pauley, Bob Hannegan and several others were there. They began to put pressure on me to allow my name to be presented to the convention. I said no and kept saying it. Hannegan had put in a call to San Diego for the president. When the connection was made I sat on one twin bed and Bob on the other. When the president used the phone he always talked in such a strong voice it was necessary to hold the phone away from your ear to keep from being deafened. I could hear both ends of the conversation.

Finally Roosevelt said, "Bob, have you got that fellow lined up yet?" Bob said, "No, he is the contrariest Missouri mule I've ever dealt with." The president then said, "Well, you tell him if he wants to break up the Democratic Party in the middle of a war that's his responsibility" and bang up went the phone.

To say I was stunned is to put it mildly. I sat for a minute or two and then began walking around the room. All the people in the room were watching me and not saying a word.

Finally I said, "Well, if that is the situation I'll have to say yes, but why the hell didn't he tell me in the first place."

pick it quickly. I sat for a minute or two and then began walking around the room. All the people in the room were watching me and not saying a word. Finally I said "Well, that is the situation. I'll have to say no, but why the hell didn't you tell me in the first place."

Then we had difficulty finding someone to nominate me. Finally all my friends that I had asked as a candidate

to hold the place open for your own to keep from being deadset. I could lean both ends of the convention. Finally Roosevelt said, "But have you got that fellow lined up yet." But I said "No, he is the convention chairman and he does that stuff." The President then said "Well, I've got to tell him of to start to hook up the Democratic Party in the middle of a war. That's his responsibility and hang up next to the place." To say I was staggered is

Then we had difficulty finding someone to nominate me. I'd told all my friends that I was not a candidate and they were committed to someone else.

We finally persuaded Senator Bennett Clark to do it.

When the Missouri delegation to the convention met, someone offered a resolution endorsing me for vice president after I'd been elected chairman of the delegation. As chairman I ruled the resolution out of order as I was not a candidate.

About that time someone called me to the door to pass on the admission of some visitor and Sam Wear, vice chairman of the delegation, put the motion and I was unanimously endorsed by the Missouri delegation to the Democratic convention of 1944 for the nomination as vice president of the United States.

In times gone by the Missourians at Democratic conventions were always in a knockdown and drag-out fight over what they'd do. That was so in 1896, 1912, 1920, 1924, 1928, 1932. But this time there was no fight over the chairman or the man they were for. I didn't understand it.

Sometime after my break with Byrnes I learned that President Roosevelt had called a meeting at the White House of the political leaders in the party to discuss the situation with regard to the nomination of a vice president at the coming Democratic convention.

Bob Hannegan, Ed Pauley, chairman and treasurer of the National Democratic Committee, Frank Walker, postmaster general, the president's son-in-law Colonel Boettiger, George Allen, Ed Flynn and one or two others were there. Wallace, Douglas, Jim Byrnes and Truman were discussed. After some acrimonious debate the president told them that he thought Truman would be the best candidate. He gave Hannegan a note in longhand which said, "Bob, Truman is the man. F.D.R." He also told

Frank Walker to inform Jimmy Byrnes of their action and his decision and to tell him he was out.

It is my opinion that Byrnes knew of this action when he called me in Independence. I knew nothing of the meeting until long afterwards.

All the Democratic senators on my Committee to Investigate the National Defense Program had urged me at one time and another to come out for vice president. I always refused and would ask the one to whom I was talking to name four former vice presidents who were not alive. Not one could do it. I also would tell them that I was perfectly happy in the Senate and that I wanted to stay there.

Some time after I became president one of the radio shows asked a sixty-four-dollar question which was to name the living vice presidents. The person asked named all of them but me!

After the nomination and my return to the hotel with police and secret service none of us was happy. But we all faced the situation and have been facing it ever since.

In the fall of 1944 I went to the Legion fair at Caruthersville as usual and then drove to Mississippi with Fred Canfil. My objective was to see my nephew J. C. Truman, who was training at a naval camp west of Gulfport. We stopped in Gulfport and I saw my nephew. Then we drove to Biloxi and called on Mr. & Mrs. Luxich from whom we'd rented a cottage some years before. Margie had a strep throat when she was about eight years old, which affected her heart. Our good child doctor, Wilson by name, said that sea level would cure the ailment. So we drove to the Gulf Coast, rented a cottage, and the cure was complete.

After calling on the Luxich family and J. C., Fred and I started for New Orleans. We stopped at Pass Christian for lunch and had fillet of flounder. It was excellent. Mr. Luxich used to take Margie out into the Gulf when we first

93

"After the nomination and my return to the hotel with police and secret service none of us were happy. But we all faced the situation and have been facing it ever since." [Margaret and Mrs. Truman at the Democratic National Convention in Philadelphia, 1944.]

went to Biloxi. He had a gasoline torch and a broomstick with a nail in the end of it, and would spear flounders.

Those that Canfil and I had at Pass Christian on the way to New Orleans were as good as I ever tasted.

We arrived in New Orleans and put up at the Roosevelt Hotel. I went to see a banker friend of mine and that night spoke to the Mississippi Valley Association on the Missouri Valley Authority. All I received was a vote of no confidence!

The next day we boarded a Southern Pacific train and began a cross-country tour. Beaumont, Houston, San Antonio, Uvalde where I had a grand visit with Mr. Garner, El Paso, Tucson, and finally Los Angeles. Then to San Francisco, Portland, Seattle and across the northern part of the country on the Chicago, Milwaukee and Pacific railroad. Stopped at all the towns of any consequence, told the newspaper at Spokane what a lousy sheet it is, addressed a labor conference and then went on east. That trip was the first "whistle stop" campaign. . .

CHAPTER IX

President of the United States

(An Undelivered "Farewell Address")

F ive days from today, at twelve o'clock noon, January 20, 1953, I shall transfer the burden of the presidency and return to Independence, Missouri, a free and independent citizen of the greatest republic in the history of the world.

Thirty years ago, on January 1, 1923, I took the oath of office, assuming the responsibility for a county office to which I had been elected. I have been in elective public office continually except for two years since that date—thirty years.

It is a long time—but for me a happy one. My daughter was born in the year I suffered my only personal political defeat. Two years later I was back in the harness and have served continuously since—as executive of a county of 600,000 people, U.S. senator from a great state, vice president of the United States, and since April 12, 1945, president of this great country.

The last seven years and nine months has been a period without a dull moment.

About five o'clock on the afternoon of that fateful April 12, 1945, the senate recessed and I walked over to the office of the speaker of the house, Mr. Rayburn. I was informed as soon as I arrived that Mr. Early, the press secretary of the president, wanted me to call the White House. As soon as I could talk to Mr. Early, he told me to come to the White House as quickly as possible, to come in by way of the Pennsylvania Avenue entrance, and to come to Mrs. Roosevelt's study.

When I arrived I was informed that the president had passed away. It was a real shock when Mrs. Roosevelt made the announcement to me. The secretary of state came in immediately and after offering to do anything I could for Mrs. Roosevelt, I told Mr. Stettinius to call a cabinet meeting.

I was sworn in as president at 7:09 P.M. by the chief justice of the United States, Mr. Stone.

Things began to happen at once. The meeting of the United Nations had been called for April 25. I was asked if that meeting would go forward. I announced that it would.

After attending the president's funeral, I went to the Congress with a message. On May 7, Germany surrendered. The announcement was made on May 8, my sixty-first birthday.

Mr. Churchill called me shortly after that and wanted a meeting with me and Prime Minister Stalin of Russia. Later on a meeting was agreed upon and Stalin, Churchill and I met at Potsdam to implement the agreements made at Tehran and Yalta.

At the time, the Potsdam meeting was considered a success. Russia agreed to enter the Japanese war, the use of the atomic bomb was decided. We came away from the meeting feeling that we were well on the road to world peace.

The bomb was dropped on Japan and Japan surrendered. Russia began to break agreements made with Great Britain and the United States, one by one. We had trouble in Iran, in China, in Greece, in Italy, in France, with the communists. Russia was at the root of all these troubles.

In early 1947, we decided on help to Greece and Turkey. Then came the Marshall Plan which had been discussed at Cleveland, Mississippi on May 8, 1947 and at Boston in June. Dean Acheson spoke in Mississippi, General Marshall in Boston.

Then the Russians closed the road to Berlin. We and our allies supplied Berlin by air. China folded up as a result of the weakness of the Nationalist government.

"Mr. Churchill called me shortly after [President Roosevelt's death] and wanted a meeting with me and Prime Minister Stalin of Russia. Later on a meeting was agree upon and Stalin, Churchill and I met at Potsdam to implement the agreements made at Tehran and Yalta."

All these disturbances and many more were sparks that could start a third world war. One of the worst of these was the division of India into two commonwealth countries. Another was the war between Israel and the Arabs. The two bad situations were stopped without a world conflict.

The last and worst of the lot was Korea. But if we had not persuaded the United Nations to back up the free Republic of Korea, Western Europe would have gone into the hands of the communists.

We inaugurated the Atlantic Pact, the Latin American Agreement, and the Pacific Defense Agreement, all for the defense of the free world and to strengthen our friends and allies so as to prevent their invasion by Russia.

All these events required momentous decisions by the president of the United States. He made them, and with but one idea in mind—eventual peace in the world.

In the inaugural address after my election in 1948, there was a fourth point which suggested a plan for technical assistance to free nations to help them to help themselves and to have them develop their natural resources.

Point Four is not an aid program in the sense that the Marshall Plan and the Mutual Defense Program are. It is a plan to furnish "know-how" from our experience in the fabulous development of our own resources.

Point Four was implemented and Dr. Bennett, head of Oklahoma A & M College, was put in charge. He immediately went to work and started programs in a dozen countries or more. Wonderful progress has been made in India, Turkey, Ethiopia, a half-dozen South American countries, in Liberia and other places.

Point Four will be our greatest contribution to world peace. . . .

All these emergencies and all the developments to meet them have required the president to put in long hours—

"*The last and worst of the lot was Korea. But if we had not persuaded the United Nations to back up the free Republic of Korea, Western Europe would have gone into the hands of the communists.*" [President Truman and General MacArthur meet for the first time, Wake Island, 1950.]

usually seventeen hours a day, with no payment for overtime. But it was worth the effort because results are showing.

We have 62,500,000 people at work, businessmen, farmers, laborers, white-collar people, and all have better incomes and more of the good things of life than ever before in the history of the world.

There hasn't been a bank failure in seven years. No depositor has lost a cent in that period.

The income distribution has been equitable and fair to all the population.

Many things have happened. The White House very nearly collapsed, the country has been through four campaigns, two congressional (1946 and 1950) and two presidential (1948 and 1952).

I have been to Mexico, Canada, Brazil, Puerto Rico and the Virgin Islands. Wake Island and Hawaii. I have visited every state in the Union but Vermont. Traveled 135,000 miles by air, 17,000 by ship, and 77,000 by rail, but the mail always followed me and wherever I happened, there the office of the president was.

I sign my name on the average 600 times a day, see and talk to hundreds of people every month, shake hands with thousands every year, and still carry on the business of the largest going concern in the world.

I wish my successor every happiness and success.

For the first time in the history of the executive branch an orderly turnover is being made. I have briefed my successor completely on all the affairs of the country, both foreign and domestic. All cabinet officers have been briefed, as well as new heads of bureaus where they have been appointed. It has never been done before when the newly elected president has been of the opposite political party.

Mrs. Truman and I are leaving the White House with no regret. We've done our best in the public service we've rendered.

The sturdy, rebuilt White House will stand for centuries, as will the country itself. We feel we've made a contribution to the stability of the U.S.A. and the peace of the world.

CHAPTER X

Independence, Missouri

(Notes for a Speech, February 5, 1953)

"I've been taking my morning walks around the city and passing places that bring back wonderful recollections."

Appreciation for this gathering, the one at the Washington Union Station, at stations along the way, through West Virginia, Ohio, Indiana and Illinois.

Wonderful reception at St. Louis, Washington, Missouri, Hermann, Jefferson City, Tipton. Then the climax of all the trip home at the R.R. depot in Independence, 9,000 or 10,000 friends and neighbors there, 5,000 at the front gate at 219 North Delaware.

Mrs. T., Margie and I have been through all the trials and tribulations of public elective office from eastern judge in the election of 1922, presiding judge in the election of 1926, U.S. senator in 1934 and again in 1940. 1940 was a vicious personal smear affair. Then 1944 and 1948, both rough, tough affairs, as was 1952, a campaign for someone else.

There were rough times of service, locally, in the senate and as president of the United States, the greatest office in the history of the world—the greatest honor and the most awful responsibility to come to any man.

But that home town reception was worth all the effort, all the trials. Never has there been anything like it in Independence or any other ex-president's home town.

I can never express to you adequately the appreciation of this family.

I've been taking my morning walks around the city and passing places that bring back wonderful recollections.

The Presbyterian Church at Lexington and Pleasant Streets where I started to Sunday school at the age of six years, where I first saw a lovely little golden-haired girl who is still the lovely lady—Margie's mother.

I pass by the Noland School where I first went to school in 1892. Had a white cap with sign across above the cap's visor, which said "Grover Cleveland for President and

Harry S. Truman home in Independence, Missouri.

Adlai Stevenson for Vice President"—the grandfather of the man I supported in 1952 sixty years later.

Just south of this building stood the old Columbian School, which was brand-new when I was ready for the third and fourth grades.

The Ott School over on Liberty and College where I was in the fifth grade under Aunt Nanny Wallace—Bess's aunt.

I pass the site of the old Independence High School at Maple and Pleasant. Ours was the first class to be graduated there, in 1901—fifty-two years ago.

And so it goes. What a pleasure to be back here at home—once more a free and independent citizen of the gateway city of the old Great West.

Our grandparents were citizens here in the county when the going was rough. They were real pioneers. They gave us our background of honor and integrity. I hope we've lived up to that heritage.

Thanks again, home folks, for a most happy return.

CHAPTER XI

Random Thoughts in Retirement

"Readers of good books, particularly books of biography and history, are pre-paring themselves for leadership. Not all readers become leaders. But all leaders must be readers." [President Truman speaking to a school group, 1960.]

On Reading

Readers of good books, particularly books of biography and history, are preparing themselves for leadership. Not all readers become leaders. But all leaders must be readers. Many readers become historians and teachers. They are retiring, timid when publicity is involved, and are among the greatest assets to this republic.

Political leaders like publicity. It does them little good unless the historical background is there to support the publicity. No one ever loses by reading history, great literature—and even newspapers.

On Politics and Politicians

Politics in our free country is "Government." The Tenth Amendment to the Constitution of the United States provides that "The powers not delegated to the United States by the Constitution, nor prohibited by it to the States, are reserved to the States respectively, *or to the people.*"

That last phrase implies that all powers of government under the Constitution of the United States come from the people, and unless the people delegate those powers to the executive, the legislative, and the judicial branch of the government, then the powers of government remain with the people. The implication is there, too, that the people may revoke granted powers by certain procedures. Hence politics is "the science and art of government." Under our Constitution the "art of government" is the art of understanding and working for the interest of the people.

The good word "politics," which really means the science of government, has been abused in our time, and has been given a definition meaning "dishonest management to win an election for a party or a candidate." The use of the latter definition by newspapers and those who like to turn their noses up at everyday people has obscured the real meaning of the word "politics."

A politician is a man who is interested in good government. There is a saying in the Senate that a statesman is a dead politician. A statesman must be an honorable man and he must be a good politician in order to become a statesman under our form of government. If you will study the history of our country you'll find that our greatest presidents and congressional leaders have been the ones who have been vilified worst by the current press. But history justifies the honorable politician when he works for the welfare of the country.

I would risk my reputation and my fortune with a professional politician sooner than I would with the banker or the businessman or the publisher of a daily paper! More young men and young women should fit themselves for politics and government.

What Will History Say?

I have always believed that right will prevail in the end. It has been a policy with me to get the facts and then make a decision. That decision should be made in the public interest as conditions then prevailing require. If the facts available justify a decision at the time it will also be correct in future time.

It is not possible for a public man to be constantly worrying about what history and future generations will say about decisions he has to make. He must live in the present, do what he thinks is right at the time, and history will take care of itself.

As an administrator in local government, as a United States senator and as vice president and president of the United States, decisions made by me were made on the

"I would risk my reputation and my fortune with a professional politician sooner than I would with the banker or the businessman or the publisher of a daily paper! More young men and women should fit themselves for politics and government." [Robert Kennedy visiting with Truman, 1960.]

facts available. I found that some of them did not work out as anticipated, because of factors unknown at the time the decision was made. I believed in publicly admitting the error and amending the decision. No man can make a perfect score.

On Planning

When we begin to talk about planning, the opposition to a thought-out plan becomes vociferous . . . You know, when you want to confuse an issue always talk about what it will do to something that has no relation to it.

You see, our old squirrel-cap ancestors were people who could not stand restraint in any form. I once asked Harry Byrd what became of the "white trash" of Virginia. He didn't know. But the question was answered by a hired man of mine on the farm out here in southern Jackson County. He said that those people in Virginia ought to be the cream of the crop because they had emptied all the trash into Ohio, Indiana and Kentucky! He was from Grayson County, Virginia, which is that toe of the Old Dominion that sticks into Kentucky, Tennessee, North Carolina, and West Virginia.

You see, it was the nonconformists who first settled Virginia, Massachusetts, Rhode Island and Providence Plantations, New York, New Jersey, Pennsylvania, Maryland, South Carolina, and Georgia.

But as soon as they had become top citizens, slave-owners, and exploiters of cheap labor and poor people, they became aristocrats and the better element, so—the poor people and the exploited had to move on. I can remember how our Kentucky relatives used to hold their heads high and their noses up when they came to see us poor Missourians. They've changed somewhat since one of those poor relations by accident and not intention became the president of the United States. But that is neither here nor there.

What we want to discuss is plans. Personal plans, city plans, county plans, regional plans, national plans.

A man cannot make his plans for his personal future until he finds out definitely what he proposes to do with himself. I can remember when I was very young—in the fifth, sixth, and seventh grade at school, wondering what my own future would be. I was an avid reader of history and particularly the lives of great men and famous women.

I found that some were born to greatness, some attained it by accident, and some worked for it.

Most of Plutarch's and Abbott's greats were great by inheritance and position. But there were many who came from nothing to the top. Some were honorable and decent, some were unscrupulous and personally no good.

In the picture of the great in the United States, most were honorable, hardworking men who were ready when opportunity knocked. Most had training on the farm, in finance or in the military. Well, I tried all three!

When I came to the point where I could plan for a community, I had studied city and county planning. I found that Chicago had the greatest regional plan in the 1920s and 1930s. I found that George Washington had hired a Frenchman to make a plan for the capital. He'd made it, but it was thrown away, and it finally cost millions and millions of dollars to restore a small part of it. The restoration is far from finished.

It was my privilege to set up a regional plan right here and the same thing happened to it as happened to Washington's. Some of the citizens of this community are awaking to what was intended by a county judge thirty years ago. But they are like the old supreme court judge when he stated that at ninety-two the lovely ladies were smiling at him thirty years too late.

Maybe we can remedy the situation here, but you've got to have forward-looking men to do it and not men who are trying to discredit an administration that has been out of control of the city for fifteen years.

That is the trouble in Washington now on national affairs—and the president must have a national plan and not spend his time making bunglers and traitors out of his predecessors.

"Keep working on a plan. Make no little plans. Make the biggest one you can think of, and spend the rest of your life carrying it out." [Harry S. Truman and grandchildren on his last trip to Key West in 1968.]

Keep working on a plan. Make no little plans. Make the biggest one you can think of, and spend the rest of your life carrying it out.

On Opportunity

We think we are in the midst of perpetual turmoil and that the world is on the road to ruin in a hurry.

I wonder what the citizens of the Mesopotamian valley thought when Alexander came.

What did the people of Carthage think after the Third Punic War?

I wonder what the people of the great Roman Republic were thinking in the time of Marius and Sulla and when Pompey and Caesar were contending for power.

What did the people of Western Europe think when Attila the Hun was being bought off at the gates of Rome itself by Pope Leo, or what did they think when Charles Martel was meeting the Saracen at Tours?

When England was torn by the Wars of the Roses and before that by William I—what did people think of the end of all things good?

The Thirty Years War, the Seven Years War, the Napoleonic Wars brought misery and starvation to the people of Middle Europe—but the world survived.

Now we have the results of two all-out wars covering the whole world to face, and the responsibilities of the Atomic Age to assume.

If the world and its people can survive all these outbreaks, not to mention Ghengis Khan and Tamerlane, surely we are now faced with the greatest age in all history.

Opportunity—what is opportunity? Define it and go on from there.

1. boyhood home of Harry S. Truman in Independence, 1890–1896, Crysler Street

2. boyhood home of Harry S. Truman, 1896–1902, Waldo Avenue and River Boulevard

3. Mrs. Truman's girlhood home, until c. 1903, 610 N. Delaware Street; the original structure is no longer standing

4. location of Noland family home, at present location of William Chrisman Junior High School

5. Noland family home, 216 N. Delaware

6. Truman home, 219 N. Delaware

7. First Presbyterian Church

8. Woodland College; original structure no longer standing

9. Independence courthouse

10. Harry S. Truman Library

11. Noland School

12. Columbian School

13. Ott School

14. Independence High School

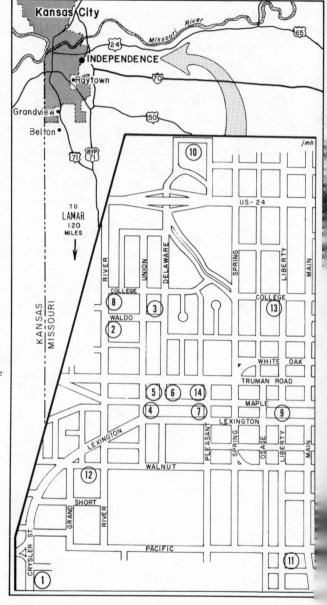

Notes

A short explanation about editorial procedure. Here there has been no change from the president's words, except for the most minor of points. Once in a while a presidential aside or digression had to be ellipsed out, and hence the appearance of ellipsis points. In a few instances the president omitted an article or turned the tense of a verb, and these errors have been corrected, without brackets. The president sometimes had trouble with spelling, which has been righted.. Lastly the capitalizations: in the name of consistency I have edited capped nouns and adjectives into lowcaps, on the principle that capitalizations appear Victorian.

It almost goes without saying that the president never arranged his autobiographical writings in chapters, and the present divisions have been made only for readability.

Photographs are from the Truman Library collection. The library possesses an enormous number of pictures, most of them 8 x 10s, and they have been sleeved in plastic and filed in some 244 archival boxes. Anyone using the collection can approach it by either of two ways. The first is a card file, carefully kept by Pauline Testerman. I have preferred not to rely on the card file, at best an inadequate description, and have gone through the photo boxes, item by item, identifying pictures that might describe the concerns of the *Autobiography*. I describe subsequently chosen photos in Truman's words, sometimes with more exact description in brackets.

The following points explain obscurities in the text—after page numbers and quotation of tailends of sentences:

(3) *in Cass County, Missouri*. Truman's early life was marked by annual moves from farm to farm, until the future president was four years old. Harry S. Truman was born at Lamar, in Benton County, and when he was one year old the family moved to Harrisonville in Cass County, where the frog-chasing incident occurred. Thence to a farm south of Harrisonville known as the

Dye Farm. In 1887 the family moved to the farm of Grandfather Solomon Young.

(3) *the S for both of them.* Ever afterward Harry S. Truman had to explain that he possessed no middle name but that the S was not an initial and stood for two names. When on April 12, 1945 he took the presidential oath of office, Chief Justice Harlan F. Stone intoned, "I, Harry Shippe Truman . . ." and the new president replied, "I, Harry S. Truman . . ." Grammarians frequently refuse to place a period after Truman's middle initial. The holder of the initial customarily used a period, but omitted it when in a hurry.

(3) *with Uncle Harrison and our Grandmother.* Here is reference to the six-hundred-acre farm to which the family moved in 1887 and remained until 1890 when the Trumans moved to Independence. After the turn of the century they moved to Kansas City and then to Clinton and in 1906 back to the large farm, where Harry S. Truman's father died in 1914. His mother lived on the farm until 1940, when a foreclosure forced her to move to Grandview. In 1946 the president gained part of the farm back, and after his mother died in 1947 he and his brother Vivian and sister Mary Jane sold off sections of this land. Most of it went to construction of a shopping center, now known as Truman Corners. The home farmhouse remains, and is about to be restored and opened to the public as a national historical landmark.

(5) *around the other six."* Uncle Harrison Young was a storyteller, and according to the president one of his tall tales went as follows:
"A pound of turnip seed will sow two or three acres. In 1901 which was a very, very dry year in our part of the country, my old Uncle Harrison Young who was operating the 600-acre farm which my brother and sister and myself afterward inherited, went to the seed store in Belton about July 20th and told the good old proprietor that he wanted to buy six bushels of turnip seed. I was with him. The store owner stepped back and looked my uncle over and said, 'My God, Harrison, what the hell you

want with six bushels of turnip seed?' 'Well,' said my old uncle, 'it's never been so dry out our way and I understand that turnips are ninety percent water and I want water, and I'm going to sow the whole farm in turnips.'" (Letter to Carol Taylor, undated; Post-Presidential Files, General File, Box 286, handwritten.)

(8) *we had a new sister.* Mary Jane Truman never married, and in her later years cared for the president's aged mother; the two women lived in a small bungalow in Grandview. Mary Jane died in 1978 at the age of eighty-nine. The president's younger brother Vivian for many years worked for the Federal Housing Administration in Kansas City, and retired to Grandview, where he died in 1965.

(9) *a cripple from her teens.* For generations the white residents of Independence were accustomed to live closely with the town's black families, who usually worked around the houses. There was no residential segregation, nor does it exist today. Missouri, of course, was a Southern state, and lily-white politically. Perhaps the president's liberal racial views derived from the peaceful nature of race relations in Independence.

(9) *superintendent of schools.* In the Midwest of long ago, any male high school teacher who gained the respect of his students and the community was known as "professor."

(12) *was Paul Bryant.* Woodland College, run by Professor George S. Bryant, Paul's father, was one of the many local educational institutions that later disappeared.

(12) *after fifty years.* The president was writing in 1951 or early 1952.

(17) *River Boulevard in Independence.* John A. Truman had plunged heavily in the Kansas City grain futures market, and his speculations went awry.

(18) *ever heard of.* One of the roomers in the Trow house at 1314 Troost Avenue was a young bank clerk from Abilene, by name of Arthur Eisenhower, brother of a future president.

(20) *the tellers and bookkeepers.* The Commerce Zoo was the tellers' cage.

(22) *the central business district.* At the turn of the century the owner of the *Star* was William Rockhill Nelson, whom Truman considered a terrible old journalistic buccaneer. Perhaps in expiation of his sins he founded the William Rockhill Nelson Gallery of Art, now one of the cultural centers of Kansas City.

(27) *vice president of the U.S.A.* Truman was writing early in 1945, before the death of President Roosevelt.

(28) *Osceola, Missouri at that time.* James Henry Lane, soldier and Kansas political leader, was appointed brigadier general of volunteers by President Lincoln in June 1861, and during September and October his "Kansas Brigade" operated against Confederate forces in western Missouri and "jayhawked" property of both Union and Confederate sympathizers.

(28) *Quantrill to go to Lawrence for reprisals.* William Clarke Quantrill, Confederate sympathizer and guerrilla chieftain, scourge to Missouri and Kansas, rode into Lawrence, Kansas at dawn on August 21, 1863 with a band of about 450 men, and pillaged stores, hotels, and houses, butchering at least 150 men, women and children, burning a considerable part of the town. In August 1862, as part of a Confederate force, his men had captured Independence, Missouri.

(30) *in error (to put it mildly).* The president refers to John Adams, John Quincy Adams, Charles Francis Adams, Henry and Brooks and Charles Francis Adams, Jr., and other historians native to New England of the later nineteenth and early twentieth centuries, who sneered at Jefferson because he defeated John Adams for the presidency in 1800, and made him out as an awkward teller of the truth and also an atheist. In the years after the Civil War the New England Brahmins, Republicans all, and adept with words, detested the political heirs of Jeffersonian democracy, in particular the Boston Irish.

(30) *Wish I'd kept a diary.* The reference is interesting, for the president liked to record events of his life and kept a diary. See

Off the Record: The Private Papers of Harry S. Truman (New York, 1980).

(31) *the little town adjoining it on the clover field.* Grandview.

(34) *political ones in my opinion.* The president was proud of his Baptist faith. He detested religious pomposity, and although Bess attended the Episcopal Church and he went there on occasion, he found Episcopal bishops especially difficult to take. Sometimes they came to his White House office to ask for this or that, and he discovered their company unforgettable, their requests usually impossible.

(34) *that makes me very happy.* Years later, in May 1931, while staying in the Pickwick Hotel in Kansas City, Truman wrote out a little essay on hotel stationery entitled "The Ideals I've Tried to Make Work and Perhaps Haven't." The essay begins with attendance at Presbyterian Sunday School: "I'd been going to the Presbyterian Sunday School since I was six. My mother had been raised a Baptist, and so had my father, but neither of them were active in the church. My mother had taken her membership out of the Blue Ridge Church because she felt that there were too many liars and hypocrites in it. So when we moved to Independence in 1890 she took us to the nearest Sunday School which happened to be the Presbyterian. I saw a beautiful curly haired girl there. I thought (and still think) she was the most beautiful girl I ever saw. She had tanned skin, blond hair golden as sunshine, and the most beautiful blue eyes I've ever seen, or ever will see. When we moved as before stated I started into the fifth grade to this beautiful young lady's aunt (great aunt). She sat behind me. I could not keep my mind on lessons or anything else. I read *sweet* stories. Always she was the heroine and I the hero. She never noticed me. I went all the way to graduation in high school with her and still she never paid me any attention except on occasion to let me carry her books home sometimes. I am still as crazy as ever at forty-seven and she is the mother of my daughter. I wish I had the power of Tolstoy or Poe or some other genius to tell it."

(34) *an eastern judge in Jackson County.* The western half of Jackson County comprised Kansas City and the eastern a largely agricultural area dominated by Independence. The "county court" was in fact the county commissioners, who looked after tax levies and expenditures on roads, poorhouses, insane asylums, courthouses. There was a judge of the court for the eastern district, that is, Independence and environs, and for the western district, Kansas City, and a "presiding judge" elected at large.

(41) *Batteries B and C into a regiment.* Truman had kept in touch with the army over the years, even though on the farm near Grandview: "After moving to the farm in 1906 my attendance at Battery drills in the National Guard was not as regular as it had been while I was working at the bank. Nevertheless I attended as often as I could and kept up my contacts with the members of the organization. When the Missouri National Guard went to the Border in 1916 the whole burden of running that six hundred acre farm fell on my shoulders and I couldn't go. It was a real regret that I didn't get that Mexican Border training."

(41) *assigned to me to operate the canteen.* The president had met Jacobson years before, when he was a bank clerk. The two men remained close friends until Eddie's death in 1955.

(45) *the* George Washington *for France.* A former German liner, the ship took President Wilson to the Paris Peace Conference in 1918, and Wilson used it for a hasty return trip in February-March 1919 and for his final trip home in June-July.

(45) *became able to teach others.* The "75 gun" is the famous artillery piece with which the French equipped not merely their troops on the Western Front but the Americans. Years later, after the Second World War, one of the last of these guns in the United States was presented to the Truman Library in Independence, where it is now on exhibit.

(46) *all continue to call me Captain Harry.* The president's papers in the Truman Library contain hundreds of letters to and from

the old comrades, written over many years; the affection between the captain and his men was boundless. In the inaugural
parade of 1949 the old veterans occupied a place of honor. At
the present writing (1980) only a handful remain.

(48) *about 10:00 P.M., September 28.* Varennes long before had
passed into history as the place where in 1791 King Louis XVI
and Queen Marie Antoinette, fleeing from the Revolution, were
seized and sent back to Paris and the guillotine.

(49) *proclaiming a false armistice.* The American reporter had
heard a false rumor and cabled his newspaper contacts in the
United States. The cable passed the censor, causing a riot of
celebration, until officials of the Wilson administration denied
the report.

(51) *Easter Sunday morning, April 20.* Truman returned to the
United States aboard a small former German ship, the *Zeppelin*,
a rough rider, and most of the troops making the passage were
seasick. Coincidentally, Benedict Zobrist, father of the Director
of the Harry S. Truman Library Benedict K. Zobrist, served on
the engineering crew of the U.S.S. *Zeppelin* as a U.S. Naval warrant officer, apparently assigned this duty because of his ability
to read German. When the younger Zobrist came to the Library
in 1969, he realized Truman's association with the ship and presented to President Truman a large photograph of the *Zeppelin*
which had long been in the Zobrist family. Also present at that
meeting was Edgar Hinde, Sr., then postmaster of Independence, Mo., and a member of Truman's battery. Both Truman
and Hinde reminisced about the rough trip home. Zobrist's
father recalled many years earlier that on one voyage to
America, the ship carried a number of German war brides, one
of whom gave birth to a baby girl who was named Zeppelina.
(From Benedict K. Zobrist.)

(55) *referred to earlier in this manuscript.* Truman was married in
the Episcopal Church in Independence, and afterward he and
Bess went on a short wedding trip to Chicago and Detroit.

(55) *while I was away at war.* Truman's memory was at fault here, for Harrison Young had died in 1916.

(55) *the debt right around $35,000.* Louisa Young (d. 1909) left the farm to Martha Ellen and Harrison, and cut off four daughters and another son with five dollars each. The others apparently had received money earlier, and in any event Martha Ellen and her husband John and their daughter and sons, together with Harrison, had kept the place going. The Young children contested the will, and their claims were settled by mortgaging the farm. Years later, in 1938, Martha Ellen refinanced her indebtedness by borrowing from the school fund of Jackson County. In 1940, in the midst of a tight primary fight for the Democratic renomination for senator, Truman discovered that some of his political enemies were seeking to show that he had taken advantage of the school fund, and to the then senator's consternation they arranged a foreclosure. A group of Truman's friends bought the farm in 1945, at a small profit to the fund, and arranged for Mary Jane and Vivian and the president to re-purchase it. Because of failure of the haberdashery in 1922 (for which see pp. 55-7) Truman during the 1920s and 1930s did not have an extra penny with which to rescue the farm.

(56) *in the latter part of 1922.* The failure of the haberdashery is unduly abbreviated, perhaps because it was such a painful episode. Truman managed to make arrangements with his creditors, but for years almost all savings had to go toward payment of the notes.

(57) *had agreed to support me.* For Truman's relations with Boss Tom Pendergast, the boss's brother Mike, Mike's son Jim, and the rival Democratic faction in Jackson County headed by Joseph B. Shannon, see ch. 7.

(61) *remodeling of the one at Independence.* Because of the divided nature of Jackson County, with Kansas City on the western side, Independence and the rural hinterland on the east, the county had two courthouses.

(64) *the other candidate.* Bennett Champ Clark, son of the Senator Champ Clark who in 1912 contested the Democratic presidential nomination with Woodrow Wilson.

(67) *entitled to one of the senators.* Over the years a rivalry developed between the Democratic organizations in St. Louis and in Kansas City, and a modus vivendi was worked out whereby each city was entitled to a senator.

(70) *the two houses of Congress.* Truman entered the senate in 1935 and found himself among a group of pretentious men, most of whom ignored him. He was a freshman senator, and some of the coldness occurred for that reason. He was considered only the mouthpiece of Boss Tom Pendergast; some wags dubbed him the senator from Pendergast; one critic remarked that Truman would have calluses on his ears, listening on the long-distance phone to the boss in Kansas City; another interpretation was that he was Pendergast's bellhop. Most senators ignored him, save for two or three kindhearted men, among them Senator Burton K. Wheeler of Montana. Thereafter Wheeler, who was sometimes a maverick, could do no wrong in the eyes of his friend Harry Truman.

(70) *its friends in Missouri.* In the later 1930s, Tom Pendergast's fascination with playing the horses, which cost enormous sums, together with two serious illnesses that may well have affected his judgment, made him an easy target for criminal investigators, and he was indicted by a grand jury, tried and convicted of income tax evasion. Senator Truman never wavered in his defense, and when Truman was vice president early in 1945, and Pendergast died, Truman hesitated not a moment about attending the funeral.

(73) *on the grounds of inefficiency.* Maurice Milligan, brother of the "Tuck" Milligan whom Truman had defeated in 1934, obtained the post of federal district attorney in Kansas City, with the help of Senator Clark, and launched an investigation of the 1936 city elections. Truman fought Milligan every way he could. It was natural that Milligan would seek Truman's senate seat in

1940, although his candidacy cut into support for Governor Stark and in reality assisted the incumbent.

(74) *was sent back to the nursery.* The bitterness of the campaign was evident in the attempt by some of Truman's opponents to argue that his middle name was Solomon and he was Jewish. Truman ran for his political life in 1940, and won, and thereafter every seemingly impossible political cause or contest did not bother him. In the campaign of 1948, when Democratic party chieftains were lukewarm to Truman's nomination, when adherents of former Vice President Henry A. Wallace formed the Progressive party, and Southerners grouped themselves around Governor Strom Thurmond of South Carolina in defense of their version of civil rights, when the Republican party nominee, Governor Thomas E. Dewey of New York, hardly bothered to campaign, and the pollster Elmo Roper announced that science had declared Dewey the winner and therefore stopped taking polls well before the election—at this dark time the president recalled his problems with Governor Stark in 1940 and took heart and fought his way to victory.

(75) *the bitter Missouri election campaign was on also.* The veritable foundation of Truman's political career was his ability to work hard, and here is an evidence of that primeval trait—he made a 30,000-mile trip around the United States, driving his own car, at a time when automobiles were not easy modes of transportation because of their lack of physical comfort and the nation's still inadequate road network. And he made the trip at the same time he was running a desperate race for reelection in Missouri.

(75) *the expenditure of $25 billion.* Years later, in 1948-1950, James F. Byrnes broke with Truman politically, but it is interesting that this account written early in 1945 displayed some feeling.

(82) *Then I had my first contacts with T. J. Pendergast and Joseph B. Shannon.* Here Truman's memory varies, for earlier he had written (p. 59) that during his term as judge from 1923 to 1925 he had dealt with Tom Pendergast and Joe Shannon.

(83) *and then he supported me.* Under Judge Truman there were two bond issues, one in 1928 for $6,500,000 and the other in 1931 for $7,900,000. In handling the ensuing contracts Truman was scrupulously honest. Fortunately he had no trouble from Pendergast, who needed an honest man in local government, and respected Truman's rugged independence. But the equation was awkward, for Truman possessed only one vote in a three-man court, and at any time Pendergast could have enlisted the other two judges and outvoted him. In apportioning the money from the initial bond issue, Truman resorted to trickery, having observed that the two judges "used to shoot craps while court was in session down behind the bench while I transacted the business. . . . when I wanted something done I'd let Baer and Vrooman start a crap game and then introduce a long and technical order. Neither of them would have time to read it and over it would go. I got a lot of good legislation for Jackson County over while they shot craps." At the same time some compromise was necessary, and about $1,000,000 in general revenue slipped away to the grafters—a necessary price, Truman uneasily calculated, to keep their hands off the $6,500,000 bond issue. (Undated manuscript entitled "More Character Sketches," on stationery of the Pickwick Hotel, probably written sometime in the early 1930s; President's Secretary's Files, Box 334, "Longhand Notes, Harry S. Truman, County Judge.")

(87) *not a candidate for vice president.* It is a maxim of American politics that the office must come to the man, not the man to the office, and this old saw has produced enormous confusion in American politics and probably confused great numbers of historians and political scientists. As one might suspect, many Americans have been ambitious for office, high and low, and the business about not seeking it has forced them into the most tortuous maneuvers to get the office—somehow they must arrange for their future in ways that do not show ambition. But in the case of Truman and the vice presidency there is every evidence that he did not seek the post. One of the members of his office staff was actively involved in plotting to get the nomination for the then senator, and Truman told him to "cut it out." The

treasurer of the Democratic national committee, the California oilman Edwin W. Pauley, a close friend, conducted an extraordinary intrigue to discredit Vice President Wallace, who wanted renomination in 1944, and discredit Byrnes, at that time President Roosevelt's "assistant president" in charge of the home front. Pauley went to the length of plotting with the president's left-hand man, his military aide, Major General Edwin F. (Pa) Watson, to remind the president deftly, on any and all occasions that the party regulars hated Wallace, that Byrnes would not do because of his dislike by labor leaders and because he was a renegade Catholic (he had converted to Episcopalianism), and that Truman was the man. Later Pauley confessed his activities in a remarkable memorandum that was used by Jonathan Daniels in *The Man of Independence* (Philadelphia, 1950), pp. 232-254, and is now part of the files of the Truman Library (President's Secretary's Files, Box 321, "Political, Vice Presidential Nomination, 1944"). There is no evidence that he had Senator Truman's support, and indeed the way in which Pauley moved to shield his activities indicates that Truman could not have been behind them. The independent-minded Truman liked the senate and was without ambition for the presidency—even though, like all individuals of the time in the upper reaches of American politics, he knew that Roosevelt was an ill man and probably could not survive a fourth term. For the Byzantine maneuvers by which the party regulars pushed Truman into the vice presidential nomination during the 1944 convention in Chicago, see the unpublished essay by Douglas D. Small, "The Choosing of a President," a senior honors thesis written for the department of history at Indiana University in Bloomington in the spring of 1980.

(89) *the ticket for vice president.* Robert E. Hannegan, Democratic leader from St. Louis, had been successively collector of internal revenue for the St. Louis district, commissioner of internal revenue in Washington, and in 1944 national chairman of the Democratic party. His urging of Truman for the vice presidential nomination might have seemed an arrangement by the senator from Missouri. There is no evidence that such was the

case. President Roosevelt had asked Truman to be national chairman, and he had demurred, suggesting Hannegan. Pauley then had gotten to Hannegan, though the task was easy for Hannegan disliked Vice President Wallace and was no supporter of Byrnes. Unfortunately Hannegan died a few years later, and his widow burned his papers.

(89) *"Bob, it's Truman. FDR."* Truman also remembered this note as "Bob, Truman is the man. F.D.R." (p. 98). It has never come to light, though some years later President Truman wrote Mrs. Hannegan and asked her to search through her papers. The only surviving note, handwritten and then typed, mentions the names of both Truman and Associate Justice of the Supreme Court William O. Douglas—Truman's name fortunately being first in both versions. President Roosevelt was appallingly careless in designating his vice presidential running mate, and seems to have believed there was no problem with his health. Or, as Truman's counsel during the presidential years, Clark Clifford, said at a recent conference at the Truman Library, Roosevelt believed he would never die. (Conference of May 1-3, 1980, sponsored by the Truman Library Institute.)

(93) *to Mississippi with Fred Canfil.* Truman's old friend and political righthand man in Missouri, Canfil, was a federal marshal. In the summer of 1945 the president took him to the Potsdam Conference and introduced him to Stalin as "Marshal Canfil," and Fred received a considerable attention from members of the Soviet delegation.

(95) *on the Missouri Valley Authority.* For years Truman had urged a Missouri Valley Authority, patterned on the Tennessee Valley Authority.

(102) *to prevent their invasion by Russia.* The North Atlantic Treaty Organization of 1949, the Rio Pact of 1947 (effective in 1949), the Japanese Peace Treaty of 1951 and its surrounding agreements.

(104) *two presidential (1948 and 1952).* In Truman's second term it proved necessary to refurbish the White House in a drastic

way, by virtually pulling the old building apart and reconstructing it. Indeed there was some sentiment in favor of knocking down even the outside walls—which, however, were kept standing, so as to give a feeling that the White House was being rebuilt, not constructed anew.

(104) *largest going concern in the world.* President Truman always refused to use a mechanical pen, and would not delegate to his assistants the right to sign his name, and so a Truman signature was a Truman signature. Despite what might seem to have been an enormous number of signatures available to autograph hunters through letters sent to people outside the government, the signatures in recent years have become increasingly scarce on the market, and thereby valuable. The auction price for a typed and signed letter, not a holograph (that is, written in hand by the president), is about $250.

(119) *some were unscrupulous and personally no good.* "When I was a young boy, nine or ten years old, my mother gave me four large books called *Heroes of History.* The volumes were classified as "Soldiers and Sailors," "Statesmen and Sages," and two others which I forget now. I spent most of my time reading those books, Abbott's lives, and my mother's big Bible. . . . In reading the lives of great men, I found that the first victory they won was over themselves and their carnal urges. Self-discipline with all of them came first. I found that most of the really great ones never thought they were great; some of them did. I admired Cincinnatus, Hannibal, Cyrus the Great, Gustavus Adolphus of Sweden, Washington and Lee, Stonewall Jackson and J. E. B. Stuart. Of all the military heroes Hannibal and Lee were to my mind the best because while they won every battle they lost the war, due to crazy politicians in both instances, but they were still the great captains of history. I found a lot of heroes were made by being in at death or defeat of one of the really great. Scipio, Wellington, and U. S. Grant are the most outstanding. I was not very fond of Alexander, Attila, Ghengis Khan, nor Napoleon, because while they were great leaders of men they fought for conquest and personal glory. The others fought for what

they thought was right and for their countries. They were patriots and unselfish. I could never admire a man whose only interest is himself." (Autobiographical manuscript of May 14, 1934; President's Secretary's Files, Box 334, "Longhand Notes, Harry S. Truman, County Judge.")

Sources

v "I have been reading a book about me. . . . I guess I'll have to state the few interesting facts of my life without the introspective trimmings with which most so-called writers and half-baked essayists clutter up the printed page . . ." Post-presidential files, memoirs, Box 10, January 16, 1954.

3 "My first memory is that of chasing a frog around the back yard in Cass County, Missouri. . . . Then I remember another incident at the same farm when my mother dropped me from an upstairs window into the arms of my Uncle Harrison Young, who had come to see the new baby, my brother Vivian." Here are the first sentences in the initial section of the six-part, 8,000-word record of the president's life up to 1945, produced by Truman in 1951 or early 1952 for the book edited by William Hillman, *Mr. President.* As mentioned, the Hillman book contains an assortment of diary entries, memos, statements on this and that, the autobiographical account, and photographs by Alfred Wagg. The autobiographical material is remarkably well done, but it suffers from lack of continuity because the president composed it over several days or a few weeks, and it contains asides and other out-of-chronology commentaries that subtract from its literary value, and hence it has served as a quarry, from which to mine chunks of description about aspects of President Truman's life not covered in the basic autobiographical account that begins with the author's graduation from high school and commences on p. 15 of the present book. The account in Hillman's book was written by hand, and the manuscript is in the Truman Library, in the President's Secretary's Files, Box 334, "Longhand Notes Undated." It occasionally differs from Hillman's publication and the *Autobiography* uses the original. The Truman handwriting is rounded and clear and very easy to read. In 1901 and early 1902 young Harry Truman attended Spalding's Commercial College and his earliest surviving letter, dated July 1, 1901, is a laboriously typewritten epistle on a half sheet of paper to his

maternal grandmother and to Uncle Harrison Young, both of whom then were living on the farm near Grandview. There is no other extant specimen of Truman's typewriting and thereafter he reverted to handwriting.

3-5 "I was named for . . . Harrison Young. . . . 'I am praying to you for help, and Lord I'm not like the damned howling church members in the amen corner; if you'll relieve me of seven of these ears of corn I'll try to wrastle around the other six.'" Undated memorandum in the Truman Library, Post-Presidential Files, Desk File, Box 3. This memo was found in the president's desk in the library after his death.

5-12 "We moved from the Cass County farm to the old home of my mother's father in Jackson County. . . . It is still published by the Independence High School after fifty years." Autobiographical account, 1951-1952.

17-20 "When I graduated from high school in May, 1901, it was expected by the family and by me that there would be some chance for more education. . . . I wasn't long at the Union National Bank until I was getting $100 a month—a magnificent salary in Kansas City in 1905." Here is the first section of the principal manuscript used for the *Autobiography*. Like the Hillman account, this massive document of about 12,000 words was also handwritten. Unlike the Hillman account, which appeared in 1952, this larger memoir was published only recently, in Charles Robbins and Bradley Smith, *Last of His Kind: An Informal Portrait of Harry S. Truman* (New York: William Morrow, 1979). The Robbins and Smith book is an admirable volume of reminiscence. In 1953 the journalist and writer Robbins interviewed Truman in Independence and helped the former president with some articles for *The American Weekly*, five essays that appeared in September and October of that year under the title of "Mr. Citizen." Almost a quarter century later, in 1977, Robbins returned to Independence to bring together a book of memories about the man he had known, this with the aid of Truman's surviving old friends and neighbors. The result was a volume done with his collaborator of 1953, the photographer Bradley Smith, whose unposed black-and-white photos of Truman immediately after the presidency, taken in Independence and environs and during an automobile trip to Washington that summer, seem as if they were made yesterday or surely not more than three or four years ago. It was in the course of working in the Truman Library in 1977 that Robbins obtained a copy of the 12,000-word Truman autobiographical account from Lawrence A. Yates, an indefatigable student of the Truman era. The account apparently was written during Truman's vice presidency, and later typed out in triplespace for use in compilation of the president's memoirs in the mid-1950s. It did not appear in the memoirs—which were done under an inexorable schedule and omitted much material because of the need to reduce a manuscript of two million words to half a million. In publishing about three quarters of this account, Robbins broke it into fragments, interspersing them with his own narrative. The original is in the President's Secretary's Files, Box 298, "Autobiographical Sketch." It is a much more self-contained account than the narrative in Hillman's book, although it covers much the same period, stopping (as does the Hillman manuscript) in January 1945 with the beginning of the vice presidency. Its author obviously was less harried, as vice president, than was the case later when Truman wrote up the Hillman material during the presidency. Indeed the vice presidency was a sort of vacation, for it also was much less of a job than being senator from Missouri. The work as vice president, though tedious because of the monotony of presiding over the garrulous senate, was not nearly as exhausting as that of the office of senator. Truman did not have the pressing of constituents upon his time, and he must have felt some relaxation of the senatorial requirement of trips back to Independence and to all the 114 counties of the state of Missouri. One may guess that during some long-winded senatorial speeches, or perhaps in the solitude of what the new vice president was wont to describe as his gold-plated vice presidential office, the erstwhile farmer from Grandview took pen in hand and in one or two sessions wrote down the happenings of his adult life during the preceding forty-four years. Something—

and perhaps it was a feeling for the enormous rise in his personal fortunes in the past dozen years, from presiding judge of Jackson County to the senate and the vice presidency—something drove him to retrace his past. In the course of the writing he tried hard to keep the narrative orderly, for on several occasions he chided himself after excursions ("I'm off the subject," "Well, I'm off the beam again," "I'm off again"). The narrative of this autobiographical account is wonderfully straight and lends itself easily to the insertions of the editor.

20-23 "Ninth Street was doubletrack, Main northbound and Delaware southbound. . . . They played 'Hamlet,' 'Romeo and Juliet,' 'Midsummer Night's Dream,' and again at the Shubert, Robert Mantell in 'Richelieu.'" Unsent handwritten letter to Roy A. Roberts, June 12, 1950. President's Secretary's Files, Box 321, "Roberts, Roy A."

27-36 "In June of . . . [1905] Captain George R. Collins decided to start a National Guard battery of light artillery in Kansas City. . . . It would have paid two farmhands." Autobiographical account, 1945.

36-7 "Along in 1915 I met a promoter by the name of Jerry Culbertson, through one of our farmer neighbors. . . . But I always did let ethics beat me out of money and I suppose I always will." On May 14, 1934 the presiding judge of Jackson County had arisen early while in his room in the Pickwick Hotel, and taking up a piece of hotel stationery he began: "Tomorrow, today rather, it is 4:00 A.M., I am to make the most momentous announcement of my life." He was to announce for senator. "I have come to the place where all men strive to be, at my age," he wrote, "and I thought two weeks ago that retirement on a virtual pension in some minor county office was all that was in store for me." In the silence of the hotel room Truman wrote a dozen or more autobiographical pages. President's Secretary's Files, Box 334, "Longhand Notes, Harry S. Truman, County Judge."

41 "I was stirred in heart and soul by the war messages of Woodrow Wilson, and since I'd joined the National Guard at twenty-one I thought I ought to go. . . . That was worth a lifetime on this earth." Pickwick Hotel stationery, May 1931. President's Secretary's Files, Box 334, "Longhand Notes, Harry S. Truman, County Judge." See above, Notes, p. 000.

41-5 "When President Wilson declared war on April 6, 1917, . . . I helped to expand Batteries B and C into a regiment. . . . We made some excellent artillerymen out of men who'd never seen an artillery weapon until the war began." Autobiographical account, 1945.

45-6 "My mother and sister came to see me at Camp Doniphan. . . . I could just see my hide on the fence when I tried to run that outfit." Autobiographical account, May 14, 1934.

46 "I've been very badly frightened several times in my life and the morning of July 11, 1918 when I took over that battery was one of those times. . . . They took up a collection and bought me a big silver cup with a most beautiful inscription on it and they all continue to call me Captain Harry." Autobiographical account, 1945.

46-51 "Along in October, notice caught up with me that I was a captain. . . . The discharge was accomplished on May 6, 1919." Autobiographical account, 1951-1952.

55-78 "After my discharge I went back to the farm and on June 28, 1919 my wedding to Miss Bess Wallace took place—the same beautiful, blue-eyed, golden hair girl referred to earlier in this manuscript. . . . We made some thirty reports over a three-year period and due to the painstaking care with which facts were assembled and presented not one report contained minority views." Autobiographical account, 1945.

81-4 "There has been much speculation about my relationship politically with T. J. Pendergast (Tom). . . . After I was through in the county at home, several grand juries, both state and federal, went over my career as a county judge with a fine tooth comb and they could only give me a clean bill of health. That's the answer." Memorandum of January 10, 1952 published in Hillman, *Mr. President*, pp. 183-89. The handwritten original in President's Secretary's Files, Box 334, "Longhand Notes, Undated," has some differences from Hillman's text, and the *Autobiography* uses the original.

87-8 "Due to the fact that the chairman was in charge, presided most of the time at the meetings of the committee, he naturally was most often mentioned in connection with the hearings of the committee. . . . I spent a most miserable week in trying to stave off the nomination." Autobiographical account, 1945.

88-93 "As I was about to leave the house in Independence for the Chicago convention of the Democratic Party, the telephone rang. . . . The person asked named all of them but me!" Undated memorandum, written sometime after early January 1950, in President's Secretary's Files, Box 334, "Longhand Notes, Undated."

93-5 "After the nomination and my return to the hotel with police and secret service none of us were happy. . . . That trip was the first 'whistle stop' campaign . . ." Autobiographical account, 1951-1952. Hillman did not use this part of the manuscript.

99-105 "Five days from today, at twelve o'clock noon, January 20, 1953, I shall transfer the burden of the presidency and return to Independence, Missouri, a free and independent citizen of the greatest republic in the history of the world. . . . We feel we've made a contribution to the stability of the U.S.A. and the peace of the world." President's Secretary's Files, Box 51, "Farewell Address to the Nation." Published in Charles Robbins and Bradley Smith, *Last of His Kind*, pp. 106-107, 109-110.

109-11 "Appreciation for this gathering, the one at the Washington Union Station, at stations along the way, through West Virginia, Ohio, Indiana and Illinois. . . . Thanks again, home folks, for a most happy return." President's Secretary's Files, Box 334, "Longhand Personal Memos, 1953."

115-121 "On Reading" is in Post-Presidential Files, Desk File, Box 3. "On Politics and Politicians" is in President's Secretary's Files, Box 333, "Undated." "What Will History Say?" is in Post-Presidential Files, Memoirs, Box 32. "On Planning" is in President's Secretary's Files, Box 310. "On Opportunity" is in Post-Presidential Files, Name File, Box 85, "Tj-Tz."

Index

Acheson, Dean, 100
A.F. of L. (American Federation of Labor), 89
Alcott, Chauncey, 22
Alexander the Great, 120
Allen, George, 90, 92
Allen, Pete, 41
American Legion, 64
Angers (France), 45
Appropriations Committee, 68, 74, 87
Arabs, 102
Atlantic Pact, 102
Atomic Age, 121
Atomic bomb dropped, 100
Attila the Hun, 121
Auditorium (theater), 23
Aunty. *See* Simpson, Caroline
Austin, Warren, 70
Aylward, James P., 67

Baer (Judge), 133
Baldwin (Professor), 9
Ball, Joseph H., 76
Baptist, 6, 28, 127
Barkley, Alben, 83, 88
Baruch plan, 78
Battery B, 41, 81, 128
Battery C, 41, 128
Battery D, 43, 46
Battery F, 41, 43
Bell, C. Jasper, 64
Belton fair, 6
Belton Lodge 450 A.F. & A.M., 32
Bennett, John J., 102
Benton County (Missouri), 123
Berlin blockade, 100
Bernhardt, Sarah, 22
Berry, Lucien G., 43
Blackstone Hotel (Chicago, Ill.), 90

Blue Ridge Church, 127
Boettiger, John, 92
Borland, William P., 36
Boss Pendergast. *See* Pendergast, T. J.
Bothwell Hotel (Sedalia, Mo.), 67
Boureuilles (France), 48
Brest (France), 45, 51
Brewster, Ralph O., 76
Brian, Donald, 22
Brown, Sallie, 9
Brown, Tillie, 9
Bulger, Miles, 56, 61
Burleson, Dick, 45, 46
Bryant, George S., 125
Bryant, Paul, 9, 12, 125
Burrus family (neighbors), 12
Byrd, Harry, 118
Byrnes, James F., 75, 88, 89, 92, 93, 132, 134, 135

C & A, 21
Caesar, Julius, 121
Camp Doniphan (Oklahoma), 41, 45, 81
Camp Funston (Kansas), 51
Camp Mills (New York), 51
Canfil, Fred, 93, 95, 135
Cape Girardeau (Missouri), 27
Carthage, 120
Casino de Paris, 51
Cass County (Missouri), 3, 5, 36, 123
Cawthorn, Joseph, 22
Chancellor, John, 6
Chicago (Illinois) regional plan, 119
Chiles, Henry, 11
Chiles, Morton, 12
China, 100
"Choosing of a President, The" (Small), 134

147

Index

Index

Index

Truman, Harry S. (May 8, 1884–December 26, 1972): in army, 37, 41-46, 48-51, 74: as bank boy, 18, 27; as Baptist, 33-34, 127; and Bess Wallace, 34, 45, 127; birthplace, 123; breaks collarbone, 6; brother, see Truman, Vivian; cap, 109-10; as Captain Harry, 46, 48, 50, 128-29; chokes on peach pit, 6; as county judge, 57, 59-61, 63-64, 82, 133; cuts toe, 11; daughter, see Truman, Margaret; diary, 30, 126-27; has diphtheria, 8-9; has eye problem, 8; on farm, 3, 5-6, 27, 30-32, 123-24; farm debt, 55, 130; father, see Truman, John A.; as first lieutenant, 41, 43-44; graduation from high school (1901), 17; as haberdasher, 55-56, 130; heroes, 136-37; inaugural address (1948), 102; in Independence (Mo.), 8, 11, 33, 56, 109-11, 124; jobs, 17, 18, 36, 37, 57, 59; on Kansas City (Mo.), 20-23; Kentucky relatives, 116; loss of farm, 17; in mailing department, 18; as Mason, 32-33, 46, 64; maternal grandparents, see Young, Louisa and Young, Solomon; and middle name, 3, 124, 132; as miner, 37; mother, see Truman, Martha Ellen; mudhole adventure, 6; music lessons, 21; namesake of, 3; in National Guard, 27, 41, 74, 128; on national platform committee, 87; nephew, see Truman, J. C.; as oil man, 37; paternal grandparents, see Truman, Anderson Shippe and Truman, Mary Jane; has pony, 6, 8; as postmaster, 36; as president, 99-100, 102, 104-05; and press, 74, 84, 95, 115, 116, 126; on public elective office, 109; results of administration, 102, 104-05; retirement,, 115-21; as road overseer, 36; salaries, 17, 18, 20; schooling, 8, 9, 11, 17, 21; as senator, 68, 70-76, 78, 131; signatures, 104, 136; sister, see Truman, Mary Jane; attends Sunday School, 33, 34, 127; as timekeeper, 17; travels as president, 104; at twenty-one, 27; uncle, see Young, Harrison; as vice-presidential nominee, 87-90, 92-93, 95, 133-35; wedding, 55, 129; wife, see Truman, Bess Wallace

Truman, J. C. (nephew), 93

Truman, John A. (father), 6, 8, 18, 33, 125, 127; death of (1914), 36, 124; discovers gas, 11; as farmer, 30, 31; as road overseer, 34

Truman, Margaret (Margie) (daughter), 34, 93, 99

Truman, Martha Ellen (mother), 6, 11, 21, 33, 45, 55, 124, 127, 130

Truman, Mary Jane (grandmother), 8

Truman, Mary Jane (sister), 8, 9, 41, 45, 55, 124, 125, 130

Truman, Matt (aunt), 5

Truman, Vivian (brother), 3, 6, 18, 55, 124, 125, 130

Truman Corners, 124

Turkey, 100, 102

Twain, Mark, 55

2108 Park Avenue (Kansas City, Mo.), 18

219 North Delaware (Independence, Mo.), 109

Twyman, Elmer, 11

Twyman, Tom, 11

Tydings, Millard, 89

Union National Bank (Kansas City, Mo.), 18, 20

Union Station (Kansas City, Mo.), 22

United Nations, 100

Universal Service Law (1940), 74

Index

Photo Credits

DATE DUE			